CHRISTIAN SCULPTURE

IS VOLUME

122

OF THE

Twentieth Century Encyclopedia of Catholicism

UNDER SECTION

XII

CATHOLICISM AND THE ARTS

IT IS ALSO THE

146TH

VOLUME IN ORDER OF PUBLICATION

Edited by HENRI DANIEL-ROPS of the Académie Française

CHRISTIAN SCULPTURE

By *VICTOR-HENRY DEBIDOUR*

Translated from the French by
ROBERT J. CUNNINGHAM

Additional Material by
ELEANOR A. ANDERSON

HAWTHORN BOOKS · PUBLISHERS · *New York*

First Edition: 1968

9886

9716

CONTENTS

INTRODUCTION

Right at the beginning of this little book, I cannot evade the question raised by its title. What, after all, do we mean by Christian sculpture? Obviously, it is not enough for an artist to be a Christian for everything that he produces to be Christian, too. And it is certainly not necessary for an artist to be Christian in his heart—let alone in his conduct—for him to create a Christian work.

This remark at once gives rise to difficulties. If all true art is sincere and should speak from the heart to the heart, how can we accept as authentically religious a work which can only be so through convention, through hypocrisy or, at best, through an aim devoid of all substance? This question was recently raised again when it was noted that certain artists well known to be atheists were working for churches. To consider it fully would carry me beyond the scope of this book, but it is possible, I believe, to point out that during the Renaissance, a great many religious artists were Christians in name only. If they did not proclaim themselves to be non-believers and did not rebel against the Church, it was because such an attitude would have proved dangerous for them, and was, all in all, less acceptable then than now. But at once the objection will be raised that, in fact, the art of that period ceased to be Christian even while it was carving Madonnas.

The solution to this problem lies in the fact that the "sincerity" of an artist is not a simple matter. As a sculptor, he may really be a Christian—out of loyalty toward his work, out of respect for his subject or, finally, out of love for the faith of those he is serving. There is a kind of substitute sincerity, which is one of the mysteries of artistic activity. On the other hand, we know all too well that the road to artistic hell is paved with good intentions, and that pious watercolors of St Teresa of the Child Jesus betray an affectation that fits perfectly the popular image of that saint in the Place Saint-Sulpice art style—which is no excuse for such a style.[1] Yet there was certainly nothing affected about St Teresa's spirituality! And that is just one more proof of the mistake perpetrated in artistic matters, when too simple a connection is made between faith and good works.[2]

Assuming an equal amount of talent in two specific works of art (if such a comparison is possible), it is clear, all the same, that that work which, in its very making and inspiration, shows signs of the theological virtues of faith, hope and love as well as the cardinal virtues of strength, prudence and temperance will have a greater chance to be authentically Christian than another work. The selflessness and humility of the image-makers of the Middle Ages were not at all matters of chance. If the concept we have formed since the Renaissance of the role and powers of the artist—a concept steeped in pride and "personal glory"—was not known at all in the mediaeval period, it was probably because of definite sociological conditions in the organization of labour. The tasks of the sculptor and mason were covered by the same regulations as were those of the surgeon and barber. But such regulations were themselves the reflection of a certain mentality. Pride of individuals had no place at all, if it was a question of labouring for the glory of God or our Lady. Of course, a kind of collective pride was to be seen, but it was the pride of the city or the parish, the pride of the donating

[1] *Translator's note:* The Place Saint-Sulpice in Paris, like Barclay Street in New York City, is famous for a tasteless kind of religious art.

[2] The Reverend R. de Pury is quite correct in reminding us that "the Holy Spirit produces believers, not artists".

guilds or brotherhoods, not of the artists' studios. And that is why art historians are in despair about attributing such works to specific artists, for the identifications are all too often hypothetical.

We must not allow ourselves to be deceived by romantic notions about the holy anonymity of the Middle Ages. More tympanums and capitals than might be thought were signed during the twelfth century—often not without pride. A sculptor might himself proclaim his work an *opus mirabile*. And yet, even in such a case, it was not just an outburst of pride similar to Michelangelo's famous apostrophe to his "Moses". For the spirit of pious humility was still present. Here, for example, is a translation of the Latin text at the base of an Italian Madonna of painted wood:

> The year of our Lord 1199, in the month of January—In the bosom of the Mother, the wisdom of the Father gleams—This admirable statue was made during the tenure of the Lord Abbot Peter, through the work of Martin the priest—to it he has affectionately dedicated his love.

A signature conceived in such terms is both a dedication and a prayer offered to God.[3] In any case, even if the works of art did not carry such explicit inscriptions, there could be no doubt at all about their Christian purpose. But here, without being too subtle, we must distinguish two kinds of purpose: the one emanating from the artist's own conscience, which is the will to work for God; and a much more materialistic purpose, which is characterized by the specifically religious use of the work. These two factors are quite different.

[3] There is nothing more moving than finding again, in far later times, dedicatory phrases that are wholly mediaeval. For example, this one at Plougonvan: "This cross was erected in 1554 to the honour of God and our Lady of Mercy and His Grace St Yves. Pray to God for the dead." Or again, this example from Guimiliau, which is all the more magnificent because the carving itself speaks as if it were a living person made up of a body and a soul: *"Ad gloriam Domini Crux ego facta fui 1581"* ("To the glory of God, I this Cross, was made in 1581").

Take two extreme cases. It is bold, but not at all absurd or scandalous, to speak of a kind of "Christian" spirituality in certain Buddhist statues that have a divine majesty, peace and feeling of silence and inner calm. There is in them a danger of a syncretism lacking dogmatic consistency, of course. But nothing can prevent a Christian soul from finding, *in partibus infidelium,* works which stir not only his admiration and emotions but also his piety. On the other hand, a statue properly executed for a Christian place of worship on an officially Christian theme may be deeply irreligious and, through its interpretation, betray the mystery it allegedly portrays. Such was the opinion of a large number of people concerning Germaine Richier's Crucifix at Assy. In their opinion, to raise on a gibbet a human form resembling a praying mantis on a twig of dead wood, as that artist did, was not enough to create in everyone's eyes a sign of the redemptive sacrifice.[4]

One thing is certain: It is not absolutely necessary, or merely enough, for a work of sculpture to be Christian in *subject* to justify its being regarded as Christian. When—as might be the case from the time of the Renaissance—the Virgin Mary served as the pretext or title for the portrait of a sweet, dignified yet profane creature, and St Sebastian was used to display the muscular development of the male nude, there was either deceit or at least a misunderstanding.[5] When

[4] At the bishop's request, that bronze was removed from the church and placed in the sacristy or presbytery. A private devotion —or if I may be so bold—a select or specialized kind of devotion (what is the proper expression?), might be able to confer a true Christian value on works which may or ought to scandalize people. I should be inclined, for my part, to apply this observation not only to the Christ of Assy but also to certain puppet-like Spanish statues with their unbearable, frightful realism or to plaster figures in the Place Saint-Sulpice style. Such comparisons are not meant as a joke.

[5] The most obvious example of this tendency was the stark naked Christ by Cellini (1562), in the Escurial.

the Romanesque or Gothic sculptors carved monsters or decorative foliage, their works were certainly more Christian because they were truly working for God and their faith, by beautifying the dwelling place which a Christian community was erecting to Christ. They were making *church* sculpture, while others were working to place statues *in a church building,* which they would tend to change into the gallery of a museum or the lobby of an opera house.

In unfavourable periods, Christian art—apart from some heroic exceptions—can be Christian only in its label and in the pretence of its works. But during great artistic periods, the slightest blow of the chisel was Christian because it sprang from a Christian community. When the Romanesque or Gothic image-makers carved the signs of the Zodiac or figures from a bestiary, they were expressing the divine power and order of creation. And it is not a paradox to say that, in contrast to the pagan St Sebastians of later times, a *Christian* Hercules was carved on the façade at Fidenza—a Hercules as Christian in feeling as Samson. Those figures of Pythagoras or Donatus, wisely seated at Chartres with writing tablets on their knees, were enrolled in the army of witnesses to the truth by the cleric who designed the church's iconographic program and by the artist who carved them. They were on the outer fringe of Revelation, as were the centaurs and sirens found elsewhere in such great numbers on the outer fringe of the work of creation.

Indeed, from the end of the eleventh century to the end of the thirteenth, God was the only subject of sculpture— the story of God and His works. And whatever was not God's light was God's shadow. But, through so many centuries, the Christian vision of all things received wondrously varied interpretations. In Christian sculpture, there was never a question of anything other than elaborating forms dedicated to the interpretation of God. And that act might be conceived in the most symbolic and abstract manner as well as in the most concrete and anecdotal fashion. The "deeds of God" are the Grace of the Trinity in the world beyond all worlds. But they are also the sap rising in the trees, and the works of man; the rebellion as well as the faithfulness of the angels; the martyrs' courage; the squabbles of sinners and the struggles of saints. Thus the domain of Christian art began with formalized monograms on the sarcophagi and early tympanums and went so far as to include the popular works of painted wood we find in Spanish street processions. Such are, from the plastic viewpoint, the two extremes of this art form, which takes in all the intermediate stages and has as its supreme focus Christ, the God-man, the prince of the patriarchs and prophets, the ruler of the apostles and saints, who is shown in His three royal poses: as the Christmas babe in his Mother's arms, as Good Friday's executed criminal on the cross, and as the judge at the end of time, enthroned among the clouds.

*   *   *

Despite the necessarily brief form of this history of Christian sculpture—and, indeed, because of its very briefness—we must indicate more definitely its general orientation and its limitations.

This little book should be considered an invitation or an introduction to a real voyage to the land of Christian sculpture. For its ambition is not so much to convey information and knowledge as to communicate admiration and love and, if the reader so desires, also *understanding*. And this is not possible if the reader is not concerned, first of all, with placing himself and remaining in front of the works themselves, in their material and spiritual authenticity.

Their authenticity has all too often been compromised, scorned or suppressed. Let us not mention the irreplaceable devastations caused by religious upheavals, revolutions and wars—from Scotland to Spain and Poland—for they are only too well known. But the vicissitudes of "taste" and commercial vandalism have also caused havoc. In a quite legal way and without any animosity, Cluny, Déols and Charroux were destroyed early in the nineteenth century. Excessive restorations too have played a sinister role by mixing up the true and the false, at times inextricably. Some of the famous capitals at Vézelay are true originals from the twelfth century; others have been repaired and restored; others are copies; and still others were purely and simply designed by Viollet-le-Duc "in the style of the period" and carved by his workmen. The outside tympanum, over which I one day saw a group of visitors go into ecstasy, is merely a work of imitation. Tourists do not always know, or are not sufficiently aware of the fact that all the large statues of the western façade of Notre Dame in Paris are works of the nineteenth century, as are all the famous gargoyles perched on the balustrade of its towers. The same is true of the bas-relief medallions on the Sainte Chapelle. The statues and tympanum of Batalha in Portugal are rather poor copies. The sculpture of the cathedral of Laon and the abbey church of Saint-Denis is, to a very large degree, modern. Such pious but sacrilegious interventions are found most rarely in Spain, but they are particularly indiscreet in England and Germany. No question but that we are dealing, in such cases, with "Christian sculpture", but we should have to study it under the category of nineteenth-century art, if such works even merit our attention.

It is possible to defend works of restoration on the grounds that they have, all the same, an interest for those who wish to look at them at a distance for the over-all effect, and that they reflect the general impression of the carved decorations as they were when intact, or as they were imagined by the master builders whose task remained incomplete.[6] In any

[6] Moreover, the spirit of imitation was not completely unknown to the artists of olden times. For example, the tomb of St Hilary,

case, it is important that people not be deceived, and it is distressing to see visitors all too often accept a concept of Christian sculpture's high point based on dubious or apocryphal pieces.

Even if we are faced with a statue that has been "honestly" repaired—and by this we mean one made from the same materials as the original statue and with the same tools, which is not easy to ensure; even if the grain of the stone and the methods of attacking it were preserved in principle —some intransigent critics might still object that the harm is all the greater. For to them, the more "faithful" a conscientious and learned kind of illusion might be, the more dangerous it seems because it deceives more subtly.[7]

Nothing can replace the examination of true works of sculpture that are ancient and still in their original location.

To be in their original location is, indeed, one aspect required for authenticity, especially for Christian sculpture,

---

in the Aude region, imitates in the twelfth century the style of the Gallo-Roman sarcophagi; and the capitals of a corridor in the cloister at Elne copied, during the Gothic period, those of a neighbouring corridor that had been carved during the Romanesque period. Such cases are both the torture and delight of archaeologists.

[7] It is quite certain that, as Le Corbusier puts it, "The cathedrals were white", when erected by their builders. They were not made to be eaten away by the rain, cracked by the "illnesses of stone", blackened by smoke, dressed in lichens—or beaten to pieces by men. All the same, every man with taste and a heart feels that time, although it has taken much from them, has also, in a different way, brought much to them. No artificial patina, despite the wonders of modern techniques, can be confused with the patina of time. And why is this so moving, unless because it shows how much these "immortal" masterpieces are alive, threatened, fragile and stubborn? Like life itself, they are vulnerable, beaten and yet unconquered.

Moreover, in carrying out the exciting technical and aesthetic study required for this purpose—a study which to my knowledge has never been undertaken—it would be necessary to distinguish "inside" sculpture from works conceived for outdoors. It would also be necessary to distinguish the different materials used: marble, limestone, granite, ivory, all of which wear and age quite differently.

which is, in the overwhelming number of examples, religious art found in churches. For such work, more than for any other kind of sculpture, the museum is only a poor makeshift. And there is something disturbing in the thought that, in any case, the famous statuary from the cathedral of Strasbourg —the Church and the Synagogue, the wise and the foolish virgins, the gable with its lions in echelons comprising the throne of Solomon—is falsely presented to us, whether we admire it on the cathedral façade, where only copies are found, or in the cathedral museum (Musée de l'Œuvre Notre-Dame), where the original pieces are displayed, unfortunately robbed of their architectural function.

It is necessary—or at least desirable—to see sculpture in its original location, under the sky for which it was made: the Irish crosses on the moor, the church at Aghthamar under the harsh sun of Anatolia, the calvaries of Brittany in the country cemetery or grassy places which they dominate. We must visualize how the fourth-century sarcophagi were grouped in the burial grounds in Rome or Arles; how in St Peter's or the Church of the Gesù in Rome cupolas were gilded and perspectives arranged around the Baroque statues; and how the modest wainscotting or rough plastering of rustic chapels framed the saints of painted wood. And all this is not because of any dilettantish desire for emotionalism, but only for a better understanding, and because every meditation requires the "establishment of the place factor".

Strictly speaking, a historic study of Christian sculpture should always evoke this art in its human environment, in the place it held in those churches of "living stones" which are the gatherings of the faithful from the first century to our own time, and from Rome or Antioch to the mission lands.

It is also important not to cut sculpture off from its technical environment. Here the boundaries are rather difficult to draw. What, after all, is sculpture? Let us assume that it is the art of forms, in relief, regardless of whether such forms are "representational" or not. But if, at first glance, this domain seems rather distinct, although immense, as soon as we examine it a little more closely, the boundaries shade off into the other major arts—architecture and painting—and especially into the minor arts.

The task of architecture is to arrange the spaces set aside by man for his needs of habitation, assembly, work, adoration or burial; architecture builds. But sculpture constantly comes to dwell in architectural forms—sometimes as a parasite. The vault, arcade, entablature, column and pier, capital and wall—all have a specific, monumental function. But they are also the places graced by sculpture, which is in itself "monumental". According to the way we look at things, either of the two arts, which are closely united, enhances the other one. The architect offers the sculptor choice locations, perspectives, surfaces and depths, spaces to fill with forms and solid surfaces to hollow out. And reciprocally, the sculptor underscores and gives rhythmic accents to the mathematical design behind the proportions of a façade, the soaring lines of a bell-tower, or the curve of an apse or arcade. They are at one and the same time works of sculpture and architecture.

It is, then, quite artificial to separate a piece of decoration whose role is to be monumental from a monument whose essential need is to be decorated. We must always ask ourselves what has been the relation between sculpture and architecture in different times and places. Their symbiosis was admirable among the Romanesque and Gothic masters. Much later, a quite different kind of agreement—of a tumultuous and sumptuous nature—might be observed in Baroque art. But in the centuries before the Romanesque period in France, sculpture brought only a poor and hesitating decoration to crude walls and massive piers. And in how many sanctuaries of the late Gothic, Renaissance or Classical period are gathered together, by chance, a large number of statues (which we might be tempted to call "works of the sculptor's workbench", just as we speak of some paintings as easel-pieces), placed here and there like so many works of art and devotion! If, in such cases, the architectural function of sculpture is not quite forgotten, then it has lost its focus. Such statuary creates, to a degree, its own adventitious, monumental framework, inside of and to the detriment of the over-all perspectives. Tombs, votive chapels, roodscreens, reredos and altars—all constitute a whole flowering of forms, which are in some degree intermediaries between architecture, the immovable art *par excellence,* and the minor arts, which are essentially movable.

From the crudely worked plaques of Chabris and St Restitut to Houdon's "St Bruno" and, alas, to the many pious plaster figures of the Curé of Ars, including the Visigothic decorations, the capitals at Moissac or Vézelay, the façades of San Zeno at Verona and of Santa Maria at Sangüesa, the narrative portals of the twelfth and thirteenth centuries, the reredos of Burgundy, Flanders, Germany or Poland, the lace-like work at Brou and the elbow-rests and small seats in choir-stalls, Christian sculpture cannot be interpreted apart from the general and specific monuments with which it has been associated.

*   *   *

On the other hand, the solidarity between sculpture—the art of relief—and painting—the art of color—should not be slighted. And not only because their iconography is almost always the same, but also because sculpture, much more often than we are tempted to believe, was conceived for a poly-chrome finish. The vestiges we have of it are obviously rather rare, but contemporary records permit no doubts on this score. There are other proofs as well: traces of paint in the folds of garments and streamers, now unmarked, on which designs were once painted. Doubtless we cannot imagine realistically the portals of Aulnay or Chartres, like a gigantic page from an illuminated manuscript, all vivid in red, blue and gold colours. And doubtless also, this concept goes against a certain predilection we have for separating arts and methods. And what would happen—beneath the outer finish of paint that needs periodic refreshening—to the texture of the stone, to the sincerity of materials whose value we have only recently discovered? These are disconcerting and annoying questions for us, but they did not bother the men of former times. To paint statues, they thought, was only to give them their finishing touches.

A remarkable example of the way the procedures we regard as specifically sculptural were associated spontaneously with those of painting and inlaying is furnished by the fragments of the Cluniac portal at La Charité-sur-Loire, which dates from the twelfth century. We find an "Adoration of the Magi" in which the garments of the figures were certainly painted. The eyeballs are of inlaid black marble; the fringes and embroideries are suggested by trepanning; and there is reason to surmise that clusters of multicoloured stones were once lodged in the little holes left by the trepanning.

Whatever the case may be, nothing could be more false than to neglect the play of colours in sculpture. We must try to reconstruct such effects, even with our eyes closed, on the most famous tympanums, at Conques and elsewhere, and not quickly deplore as loud and blatant the reredos and statues whose colours have been preserved or restored. Only during the Renaissance was the law banning colour imposed, for the simple reason—an overly simple reason—that the works of antiquity which were feverishly adopted as models no longer showed any vestige of their original painting. Nevertheless, polychromed work was enthusiastically retained, especially in Spain. And we discover sufficient reason not to regret this fact when we see what gloomy, huge "pieces of machinery" certain reredos of the fifteenth or sixteenth centuries look like today if they are scraped down and waxed.

*   *   *

The techniques of sculpture involve two major divisions. The first consists of removing from a rough, hard block—stone, wood, ivory or gem—whatever needs to be eliminated to liberate the form. The second, on the other hand, begins with a malleable material, either directly, such as clay or wax, or through two processes, such as bronze poured into its mould of earth or sand. The first technique begins with a whole, which must be hollowed out; and the second with a space which must be filled in.

It is clear that the difference in methods brings about, in the handling of the volume, different results, which are accentuated even more by the difference in materials. On the same scale and with a similar subject, there is always a variance between the cameo and the coin, however close their relationship may be.

The distance cannot be crossed—even though this was not clearly realized—between a mediaeval statue which was little by little "discovered" in a block through blows of the chisel, and a modern statue which the artist has liberated from the block almost automatically, following the measurements of a model fashioned in clay. Waverings, errors, confidence, virtuosity, clumsiness—all these factors cannot be translated in the same way. Some critics, particularly sensitive to the high spiritual value of the fairest sculpture of the past, have attributed it in part to the very procedures of its creation. And doubtless, the servitude and grandeur of this craft are more powerful and elating when the carving is done directly. They contribute more both to the humility of the work and to its majesty. The material achievement is inseparable, in this instance, from the moral virtue of the workman's integrity. It is not necessary to go so far as to say—as some have done in pushing things to the point of absurdity—that concrete is a "devilish" material because it is only produced by smashing and grinding up God's stones into a formless mishmash.

Yet all the same, the "resisting block" imposes on the artist a noble attitude. There is a mysterious analogy between his technical effort and his moral and spiritual effort.

In the church at Villeneuve-lès-Avignon, there is a much-admired ivory Virgin from the fourteenth century. The statue's leaning posture is full of grace. The Virgin draws back slightly her face and upper body as if to be able better to see and smile at the Infant Jesus, and at the same time, she holds Him close to her. And we note that this display of exquisite shading in tenderness is caused by the natural curve in the elephant's tusk. Did the artist perhaps rage against the constraint this imposed upon him? Perhaps he did not *want* to bend his Madonna in that way? But because the ivory wanted it so, he wanted it too, with docility and yet with authority. And working both *with* the element and *against* it, he made his masterpiece. Behind the lesson of "fine workmanship", is there not a lesson in holiness which the image-maker gives us unintentionally? For is it not the Christian vocation to redeem and reconcile nature—which is rebellious against the appeal of the supernatural—to a spirit of humble, stubborn and *sovereign* obedience? A misfortune opens the path for grace. In this connection, how can we not but think of the *felix culpa*?

These observations, needless to say, are not meant to attribute some kind of religious monopoly to direct carving! But it is certainly not by chance that such a method of sculpture, throughout history, has generally been closely associated with it.

It is a fact that religious sculpture ought to adjust itself less than any other kind to the easy terms and uniformity

of mass production, because religious sculpture is, by its
express aim, a thing of the soul, and every soul is new and
irreplaceable, bearing the seal of its own uniqueness. It
is foolishness or bad faith, said Ghéon, to claim, like Gide,
that every perfect Christian is "decharacterized" through
conformity to a common model. It would not be possible to
"pour the *Acta sanctorum* into an ordinary mould". Now the
more docile the material to be carved, the more irresistible
is the temptation to deviate into commercial production. An
easy production becomes both swift and cheap; this leads to
an increased demand and, as a result, to an acceleration in
the supply. The bad results of this procedure in plaster and
stucco have already been noted. But even alabaster, a hard
but homogeneous material, without snares and almost wax-
like, has sometimes lent itself to a cheapening process. The
English alabasters of the fourteenth century are examples of
the popular art of their period.[8] And this, by the way, allows
us to form a judgement of the two periods.

On the other hand, a material that has its own will and
whims and knows how to win respect for itself, instead of
degrading the artisan as he works, invites him all the more—
whether he wishes it or not—to be an artist. By being less
accommodating to the artist's slightest effort, such a material
helps him more to give the best of himself. And in this way,
it better shapes the taste of the faithful, instead of deforming
it.

It is not to be denied, however, that Christian sculpture,
even in its best periods, maintained itself by means of
repetitions and imitations. And this took place in many
different ways. It is not just that the great works were copied,
and that the important studios were centers from which
emerged artists of limited originality and slight inspiration
who would repeat themselves. We should recall that the

[8] *Translator's note:* The original speaks of "les sulpiceries" and
"le kitsch"; see Footnote 1 concerning Place Saint-Sulpice.

makers of sarcophagi at Rome, Arles and Ravenna, even in their day, used to have their workers carry out decorative patterns which had become almost automatic. But even in the most distinguished compositions, there was room for the trite and the banal. The carving of modillions, for example, was usually left by the master-builder for beginners or poorly talented workers. And as a result, such works are often monotonous even in their variety. But here we are dealing with a work of no particular religious value. It was quite a different affair, not just with the masterpieces, but with the capitals of the nave and of the cloisters, and even with the statuettes and ivories of the later Middle Ages. Even in their monotony, they are varied.

*   *   *

It will not be possible to include in this work everything that has to do with the art of relief; moreover it would not be desirable to do so. The art of working gold and silver, and the art of carving gems, by their very aim, are beyond sculpture, although some interesting connections between them might be pointed out. A study of Christian sculpture necessarily avoids art objects such as chased work, embossed metal and ivories. But here arises the matter of dimensions. Countless ivory plaques of the fifteenth century are like minuscule polyptics or portable altars—objects of private devotion which are also works of elegance, almost like trinkets. The social character of true religious sculpture has completely disappeared from such works. Their "edifying" subject matter—the Crucifixion, the Virgin and Child, or the saints—is not enough to distinguish them from profane works, such as jewellery, mirror cases or small coffers which, more-over, were often decorated in the same way. By Christian sculpture we mean, first of all, sculpture intended for and presented to the people of God in congregation—not sculpture hidden away in lordly oratories and private homes.

At this point, the different lines of thought we have just traced are seen to converge. When, we may ask, are works of gold, silver or bronze authentic and powerful forms of Christian sculpture? The answer is, first, when—like the statue of St Foy at Conques, the reliquaries in the form of busts, or the figured shrines—they serve as central points for the religious fervour of large groups of people, even though critics may be justified in regarding such works as inept and theologians in considering them suspect. And secondly, when works of bronze, like the doors of San Zeno in Verona and at Novgorod, attain a monumental grandeur as portals to the house of God. On the other hand, there is an inferior religious quality about the sophisticated statues in the votive church at Brou. Can we not say that this is due to the impression we receive of this church as a private mortuary chapel raised to the scale of a cathedral nave? The result is a double malaise created by aristocratic bombast combined with an equally aristocratic fondness for miniature art.

Christianity is a religion of man's innermost heart, and by this very fact, it is not conceivable that any of the most delicate and intimate feelings of the soul should escape the art serving that faith, if such art is worthy of it. But Christianity is also a communal faith, and on that score, its art has a tendency and a calling, in its fairest flowerings, to be formal and liturgical. This is particularly so for sculpture, which did not make its appearance until the fourth century, when the new religion could show itself openly, protected by an official status.

The role which the established powers—both civil and ecclesiastical—have had in Christianity's expansion for the purpose of promoting, guiding and financing, has been an important factor for good and sometimes for ill, from

Byzantium to Cluny, from Rome to Versailles. And it is curious to note the contradictions of our own time in this regard. To the bourgeois nineteenth century, as a general rule, religion was something private—something sacred, like private property. Hands off! Christendom was a concept to be sought only in the past, with the curiosity and zeal of the archaeologist. Our own twentieth century is awakening from that false view, but in a haphazard way, if not in a frenzy. In the past, formal art was also the art in which crowds of people participated. It is a paradox that our democratic society has lost such a concept. Now this is a most serious consideration; among other factors it has caused many intelligent people to have a real phobia of anything carrying the label of the "establishment". This is an entirely new attitude with respect to Christian art, and it would certainly have surprised and scandalized all the great artists of the past.

Such an attitude is, moreover, equivocal, for it may leave those who share it defenceless before other powers equally suspect and not less established, such as the powers of fashion and commerce. In this "age of the masses", we are haunted by the noble desire to be connected again to an art full of vigour which, in order to give people today the eternal message, has learned how to speak to them in a language which will grip them in their own way of life, in their own minds and in their own culture, and which will unite them and "make them brothers". But on the other hand, "living art" has evolved in quite different ways and its explorations—in order to avoid at all costs the commonplace—have resulted in formulas (not to mention "doctrines") of a systematic strangeness, sacrificing everything to impressions of shock. An infinite amount of subtlety is invested in being brutal, and an unbelievable amount of "boldness" in fleeing into the future. And the "faithful" who are being pulled this way and that display in these contests outbursts of excitement—either routine or snobbish—based on indifference. For they feel, indeed, even as they are looking at such art, that it is of no real concern to them.

Without considering in a fundamental way the issue of sacred art in our time (for this work is after all only historical in nature),[9] we should like to point out, particularly in regard to sculpture, that the artists of today seem to seek the perfection and purity of their art in rebellion or in escape from the very laws which established its existence. They have made themselves the satellites of those impossible-to-qualify myths, such as the poem of the blank page, or the novel without a plot or, in sculpture, the "absolute" fulness of forms. They are concerned with the elaboration of "solids"—or their total ejection by modelling space through arrangements of metallic wire. This sculpture beyond sculpture exhausts itself on the border of insignificance. Christian sculpture has always been an art that gives witness. But in our own day, as we twist iron wire or arrange holes in formless solids, we can only give witness, it seems, concerning ourselves or our day.

This little book is a historical sketch. Now, it is all too often forgotten that the role of history is to report on the past for the benefit of the present, not to find fault with the present and make projections of the future. If we reflect carefully on the matter, we shall see that only the past can be taught, and it alone can teach us things about all areas of knowledge. (I realize that this suggestion may seem scandalous and that I am presenting it here even though I cannot defend it.) Now Christian sculpture always wanted to be a teaching art. In order to present it without betraying its essential message, we ought to show it just as it has radiated in the world: as a discipline and exaltation of the "material" with which it worked; as a discipline and exaltation of the

[9] Cf. Madeleine Ochse, *Un art sacré pour notre temps, Je sais, Je crois,* Vol. 128.

spirit in illuminating the "great deeds" of God; as a discipline and exaltation of the soul in the love of God's gifts and plans.

*　　*　　*

One final observation is necessary. Christian sculpture, quite obviously, cannot be separated, in any period, from sculpture in general. For whole centuries, it was all of sculpture, and at other times it has remained always closely bound to the procedures, and even sometimes to the aims and spirit, of profane or secular art.

There is a risk that a history of Christian sculpture may evolve, without our thinking or saying it, as a history of sculpture beginning with the earliest period of Christianity—a subject already handled in a host of other excellent works. In order to keep a shadow of originality for this essay with respect to books to which it will owe so much throughout, I have decided to trace the panorama of sculpture in relationship to the history of souls (or rather of religious minds) and in relationship to the history of the Church.

Therefore, readers should not be surprised because I am not concerned with a strictly—and pretentiously—aesthetic study, but rather with a more humble—and one hopes more useful—work of reflexion. My aim is to trace what sculpture has been in the Christian tradition and what it has been among Christians. In such a limited space, this does not imply coverage of the high points of an artistic metaphysics nor a systematic inventory of specific works and their creators.

On the other hand, this aim does imply a treatment of the institutional, liturgical and theological aspects. What meaning has Christianity given to sculpture? What use has it made of the art? What catechetical and apologetical values has it assumed? And, to turn the question, what scandal-giving propensity has it displayed?

Christian sculpture is a long parade, sometimes timid and

almost out of sight because of the night and the crowds of people, sometimes triumphantly attracting attention because of its powers of austerity, majesty, emotion and jubilation. But that procession has always taken place among Christians, awakening in them, as the case may be, zeal or suspicion, devotion or curses. It has been and it remains, a battle-ground of Christian doctrine and sensitivity, as well as, indeed, a place blessed by stirring affirmations and the highest fusing of hearts. Apart from that, it would be only a splendid museum, more or less fictional in character, more or less covered with the dust of ages, left to the curiosity of the dilettante, the laminations of the art specialist or the meditations of the æsthete.

CHAPTER I

THE ROMAN EMPIRE

When the Christian faith was expanding and conquering the Roman world, sculpture was in a flourishing state. It was even too much so; the quality was not up to the quantity. All the cities of the Empire, according to their importance and wealth, exhibited countless figures executed in conformity with the canons and rules of Greek models. At the time of Constantine, the first emperor to authorize and give official protection to the new religion, through the Edict of Milan in 313, no fewer than thirty-seven hundred statues, including thirty equestrian figures, could be counted, it is said, in the public areas of the city of Rome alone. Now nothing in all this proliferation of sculpture was accepted into Christian art. Although Christianity quickly took over and developed for its own purposes the architectural style of the pagan basilicas, it absolutely refused to divert the pompous statuary of paganism to the service of the new worship.

The sculpture which confronted the Christians was devoted completely to the glory of the great men of this world and the gods of paganism—all of whom, moreover, were inextricably linked in devotion to Rome, Victory or the divine Caesars. If such images were visible everywhere, this was not only because of an interest in decoration but also because such statues were a religious form of political propaganda for those in power and a display of loyalty and patriotism by the subject peoples. (In the provinces, for reasons of economy, the statue of the emperor often had a movable head which could be changed when a new ruler took over the throne.)

Constantine was inclined towards Christianity, although he put off baptism until the eve of his death. Nevertheless, he had every intention of continuing to attract the same kind of prestige as the emperors of old when he erected a gilded statue of himself on the Forum. Now it seems that, after a history of refusing for two and a half centuries to give to Caesar the things that were God's, the Christians— when the complete reversal in their situation *vis-à-vis* the law might have induced them to weaken a bit in such matters —decided at least not to give to God the things that were Caesar's, namely an ostentatious display of monumental sculpture. According to early Christian belief, the word "statue" was the same as idol; and the word *eidolon* (which signifies "image" in Greek) has taken on a meaning which clearly proves this.

The pagan temple was basically the dwelling-place of a god as represented by his statue, and this statue was the god himself. In this connection the Christian apologists had two different attitudes, which even were confused at times. On one occasion, they would make fun of the stupidity the pagans showed in deifying something that was only a piece of stone, metal or wood. At another time they would become indignant on seeing the pagans worship evil spirits. If the first interpretation had prevailed, the problem of Christian sculpture would have been put to them in different, and far less abrupt, terms. If an idol was only an empty, spiritually neutral thing, it could be "Christianized", as was the case with the secular meeting-houses known as basilicas. But if the idol was wicked, if it tended to turn men's prayers not towards emptiness but towards demons, an uncompromising attitude was required.[1] In short, the belief in a kind of iden-

---

[1] A similar, very serious problem was raised for the early Church

tity between supernatural powers and their images, and the belief in the reality of those powers—all this was so strong among the masses that it was forced upon the Christians themselves. They conceded a purely religious value to the idols, in order to heap shame on that value, and they called the idols Satan's bodies just as they called the temples Satan's dwelling-places. They held the idols to be beyond retrieval as they awaited the moment when they could bring about their destruction. To this they were invited by passages in Scripture: The God of Israel never ceased to warn His people against idols made by the hand of man; in joining forces with idols, the people of God would not just be forgetting God, they would be betraying Him for ignoble, hostile powers; they would not just be allowing their faith to evaporate into thin air, but they would be prostituting it. According to the apochryphal Gospel of the pseudo-Matthew, when Jesus as a child entered Egypt—the land of idols, *par excellence*—the triumph of the true God was revealed by the instantaneous collapse of Egypt's diabolical images.

Thus, for the men of the early Church, carving an image of Christ was the same thing, in some way, as changing Him into an idol. And we shall encounter again, at long intervals, this same argument which has been often revived throughout history. But let us note at once that this argument has been especially concerned with sculpture in the round. For that kind of sculpture, during the first centuries of the Church, was so completely devoted to glories that were not of God that this seemed its very essence and definition, not just one use among many others of its possibilities. And besides, free-standing sculpture must have seemed more capable than paintings or works of bas-relief of embodying and releasing evil forms. Magical charms were practiced from early times on miniature figures, and one of the most

---

with regard to the eating of meats associated with pagan sacrifices: Was such an act indifferent or sacrilegious?

urgent tasks of the Church was the struggle against sorcery and magic.[2]

Around the end of the second century, Clement of Alexandria gave rather full testimony to the prejudices current against sculpture. For obvious reasons, he spoke only of pagan statuary, but the attack he made upon it indicated clearly that he rejected any possibility of such works being wholesome forms of art:

> Why, O vain and frivolous-minded men, have you trodden piety to the earth? . . . Your statue is of gold or stone; if you investigate the matter you find that it is earth which has received a shape from the artist. As for myself, I take care to walk on the earth, not to worship it; for it is not permitted that I should ever entrust the hopes of my soul to inanimate objects. . . . But as for you, art deceives and fascinates you to the point that you respect and even worship statues . . . The keepers of monkeys have noted that their animals are not deceived by miniature figures and dolls of wood or clay; would you, then, be worse than monkeys? . . . You have made a stage out of Heaven, the divine has become for you a theatrical play. . . . "You shall not make an image," said the prophet, "of anything that is high up in Heaven, of anything that is down below on the earth". And again, "All the gods of the Gentiles are demonic idols but God has made the heavens. . . . Let none of you deify the world, but rather seek the Creator of the world. . . ."[3]

In point of fact, the Christians destroyed the pagan statues as soon as they could. Not at Rome, where the sculptural adornments of the city remained almost intact up to the reign of Theodosius, but in the provinces, especially in

[2] As soon as Christian images were permitted, the abundance—especially in the East—of "miraculous images" was significant. Contemporary records mentioned a great many statues that spoke, moved, produced effects. It is easily understood that such accounts, when obligingly related by opponents of the iconoclasts during the great controversy over images, were able to afford excellent counterarguments to the iconoclasts.

[3] *Proteptique*, pp. 56–63 (translated by Cl. Mondésert, coll. *Sources* Chrétiennes).

Gaul, as the life of St Martin of Tours testifies. That is why many of the statues which have been discovered were broken, mutilated or buried. This was done either by the Christians in order to put them out of sight or by the pagans in order to protect them. The earliest relationship of Christianity to sculpture, we may say, was one of clear-cut and violent rejection.

*   *   *

There was, however, one technique and one form of sculpture that was quickly adopted by Christianity: bas-relief sculpture in funerary art.

Christian sculpture began as the decoration of sarcophagi. We cannot determine just when this took place. It is odd that the faith which had broken so definitely with pagan sculpture in the round showed itself to be, at the very start, most conciliatory toward the iconography associated with pagan tombs. As a matter of fact, the rather vague symbolism of immortality and peace of that iconography could be adapted. All one had to do was to give it, in one's heart, a more definitely Christian meaning. Thus the sign of the *ascia* (the stonecutter's adze) was carved on many pagan tombs, but as J. Carcopino has shown, it was used as a secret sign of adherence to Christianity in the Rhône Valley from the second century on.[4]

Of course, we should not be justified in classifying as Christian the sarcophagi decorated with pagan subjects that were sometimes re-used by members of the new faith. The decorated surface was either hammered in or hidden if it was impossible to accept its rendition of a pagan myth through a Christian interpretation.[5] The tombs were first

[4] J. Carcopino, *Le Mystère d'un symbole chrétien*, Fayard, 1956.
[5] For example, Orpheus; or Ulysses bound to the ship's mast and considered as a prototype of the Crucified Saviour who led his followers to the harbour of eternal salvation; or Ganymede and Endymion, symbols of the soul called to a heavenly home.

clandestinely Christian, then discreetly so, and finally overtly Christian.

Thus the matter of interpretation is ticklish. Was the absence of a definitely pagan decoration in a specific tomb a matter of chance or was it intentional? We see how difficult it is to determine the exact birth-date of Christian sculpture. Members of the Church would choose "neutral" subjects: pastoral scenes, or scenes concerned with ships or fishing with a net or a pole. But such scenes were—or might be—allegorical in nature, and, in the minds of those who acknowledged in their heart the gospel of the "Good Shepherd" or the "Fisher of Men", they could not be so indifferent as they seemed. In certain cases, however, there is no other basis for declaring a sarcophagus of pagan or Christian origin other than its probable date. But to determine the date, it would be important to have a clear reply to the question previously raised about the absence or presence of pagan motifs, and thus we are confronted with a vicious circle.

For example, an unusual sarcophagus was discovered at Ampurias in Catalonia. Its decorations include winged spirits, figures of the four seasons, scenes of wine and olive harvests, Silenus, Endymion—but also the figure of the Good Shepherd with the sheep on His shoulders. If we have here a statue of Hermes carrying a ram, then the work is entirely pagan. But can we completely rule out the hypothesis that this is a crypto-Christian tomb (doubtless heterodox in nature) on which the lover of Diana and companion of Bacchus might have been drawn into some farfetched allegory? Eros and Psyche have certainly been used in this way. A sarcophagus from La Gayolle, now kept at Brignoles, is a case of even keener interest. It seems that it can be definitely traced to the second century and thus is probably the oldest piece of Christian sculpture we have. Some of its themes—a fisherman, sheep, trees with birds, a teacher—might be doubtful in meaning. But a "Good Shepherd", an *orante,* or praying woman,[6] and an anchor (a symbol which, like the fish, is often found) leave no doubt but that the work is Christian in origin. As a result we have to accept an allegorical interpretation: The fisherman is Christ, the trees and doves represent Paradise and the blessed. Iconographically, this transitional work is still hesitating in form, although skilful in technique. But its most curious aspect is the inclusion of a head of Apollo, surrounded by a halo of sun-rays, and the figure of a seated man, naked to the waist, who probably represents a local deity (*genius loci*). The coming of the kingdom of God is secured, but pagan mythology still reigns! [7]

To acquire a quantitative and qualitative picture of early Christian sculpture, we must go to Rome, especially to the museum of the Lateran, and to Arles. The Roman cemeteries and those at Arles—the famous Aliscamps—contain a complete and outstanding set of sarcophagi dating from the end of the third to the beginning of the sixth centuries. In many cases, the most handsome tombs were used again in later times as burial places of saints or powerful men. When, with the coming of the Renaissance admiration revived for the works of antiquity, such marbles became collectors' items and objects of great value. Charles IX picked the most handsome pieces in the Aliscamps and intended to transport them to Paris via the Rhône, but all were lost when the barges sank at Point Saint-Esprit. Almost everywhere in Italy, southern Gaul and Spain, especially at

[6] Woman standing in prayer with arms half-raised (a figure adapted from pagan statues of the goddess Piety).

[7] In fact, pagan iconographic traditions of this type survived without interruption, in certain cases, up to the Renaissance, but they were *integrated*. In Byzantine miniatures and ivories, when an old man with a beard resembling a river is placed in a scene showing the baptism of Christ, the old man was a rebus of the Jordan, not a god of the waters. This was also true for the image-makers of the Middle Ages who gave a human form to the sun and moon.

Gerona, churches and museums contain many outstanding works of this type.

Although such works are chiefly found in the lands that belonged to the Western Roman Empire, the Eastern Empire made an important contribution to this art form. The study of inscriptions helps us to identify a great many Greek names. The tomb of La Gayolle, for example, is Hellenistic in type. The Asian cities that were centers for the expansion of early Christianity—especially Antioch, Ephesus and Smyrna—were in close touch with Italy. They even had direct contact with Gaul, as is shown by our information about the early Church at Lyons, and they were in touch also with Spain. On a sarcophagus at Ecija, in the province of Burgos, the sacrifice of Abraham and the story of Daniel are depicted, and the names of the figures are carved in Greek letters. Porphyry tombs, such as the one used for Constantia, daughter of Constantine, came from Egypt, where quarries of this stone existed. Even though the workshops were Western, the forms were to a large extent Eastern in inspiration. In this art form, as in all the others, the Roman, Gallo-Roman or Hispano-Roman sculptor invented nothing.[8] We are constantly referred to Eastern sources both for the iconographical repertory and the plastic feeling.

Christianity is a religion that preaches salvation after death. Its early sculpture is utterly illuminated by this vision. Nothing is sad, let alone macabre, in the images on the sarcophagi. Since it is funerary sculpture, it does not stop at death, which is regarded, quite literally, as only a passage —a journey towards the beyond which cannot be seen, just as a window-glass is lost to the eye in its very transparency.

There is nothing more incongruous, at first glance, than

[8] Let us note, in passing, that the only sculptural theme in the round to be found, the "Good Shepherd", is the same as Hermes carrying an offering. The few statues that depict this theme (in the museums at Constantinople and Athens and in the Lateran) are of Greek origin.

the subjects of the bas-reliefs of the fourth and fifth centuries. We have seen that there remained definite traces of
notions alien to the new faith. Certain of them are irreduci-
ble and should be attributed to the well-known law which
causes forms to survive their function both in architecture
and decoration. But as soon as we explore their symbolism
almost everything becomes clear. M. F. Cumont[9] has shown
that the pagans themselves gave a symbolical interpretation
—to be exact, a soteriological interpretation—to a host of
scenes. This rather common tendency of minds at the decline
of paganism was adopted by the Christians, just as it was
also adopted by the Pythagorean and Mithraic sects and
the followers of Isis. And it lasted until much later, when
stones of pagan origin were used, without any embarrass-
ment, as lintels or keystones of churches. We cannot be
certain that this was for plain decorative convenience and
without any hidden motive. At the outset, the faithful
showed a very strong tendency—one might even say an
imprudent tendency—to "baptize", through the subterfuge
of symbolism, themes whose background might have appeared suspect or quite unacceptable to them.[10]

Thus we can explain by transfer one whole group of art
forms. Right at the outset are all the pastoral scenes which
we see no need to refer to in the future. Next, we have the
grave, seated figure of a man holding a scroll (*volumen*)

[9] *Recherches sur le Symbolisme funéraire des Romains*, 1942. Cf.
J. Carcopino, *De Pythagore aux Apôtres*, Flammarion, 1956.

[10] Note also frequent cases of false identification during the Middle
Ages. Men who beheld everything through Christian eyes saw only
the Virgin in a feminine image (provided she was clothed). One
error of this type can be traced back to the fourth century: Eusebius
of Caesarea observed at Panaeas a bronze statue (*andrias*) of a
standing man holding a woman's hand. Commenting on this, German
of Constantinople said, "It looks like Jesus healing the woman
afflicted with hemorrhage". He used this as a point of departure in
his controversy with the iconoclasts. The statue in question most
probably represented either an emperor or the god Aesculapius.

who is no longer to be interpreted as the philosopher and man of letters of the pagan steles. Instead he has become a Christian meditating on Holy Scripture.[11] The statue of a standing man wearing a toga is no longer to be regarded as one of the famous orators of antiquity but rather as Christ teaching the Apostles or giving them His law. There was some hesitation about certain topics: For example, did a statue of a fisherman represent Christ attracting souls, Peter as fisher of men or Peter as head of the Church through whom Christ, the mystical Fish, is distributed to the faithful? Could a bearded statue of the Good Shepherd be identified as Peter rather than Christ? Such quibblings over details, however, are of slight importance.

Other subjects lent themselves to a more abstract symbolism. When we have to do with foliage, birds, vine branches laden with grapes, it will probably be impossible to determine to what extent the artist meant to suggest the heavenly Paradise, the mystical Vine of which the faithful are the branches, or just to fill out harmoniously the blank spaces on a panel. Besides, both interpretations were far from being mutually exclusive. On the contrary they complement each other if we consider that allegorical explanations were often elaborated concerning decorative motifs whose key has been lost or never known, whereas certain subjects, which were originally representational, had degenerated into arabesques drawn to an artist's fancy.

Whatever the case might be, an animal symbolism was developed for the sarcophagi. The Mesopotamian pattern of wild animals or birds, face to face, on a vase or vessel assumed a distinctly Christian meaning if a double procession of doves towards a chalice or of sheep towards a luxuriant tree could be interpreted as the faithful summoned to their redemption and eternal happiness. A famous acrostic had

[11] Another hold-over from paganism is the portrait of the deceased person or persons within a medallion (*imago clipeata*).

to do with the fish, the five letters of whose name in Greek, ΙΧΘΥΣ, became the initial letters of the expression "Jesus Christ, Son of God, Saviour"; and the fish soon became an ideogram for Christ. The anchor was also a mystical sign like the Cross, because it resembled the Cross and symbolized man's arrival in a safe harbour after the storms of life.

There were also subjects of directly Christian association. Their selection was believed to have been determined by casual, arbitrary factors until it was noted that such subjects systematically assembled around the dead person a commemoration of outstanding occasions in the Old and New Testaments when God had saved or listened to men. An ancient funerary prayer from Asia Minor, the *Commendatio animae,* furnished a list of such events which enables us, almost miraculously, to "decipher" the sarcophagi. It begs: "Lord, deliver his soul, just as you delivered Noah from the flood, Job from his misfortunes, Moses from Pharoah, Jonah from the whale, Daniel from the lions, Suzannah from calumny. . . ." Other prayers appealed to Jesus, the conqueror of human sufferings and death, who had cured the woman afflicted with hemorrhage, the bed-ridden man, the blind and lepers, and has raised up Lazarus. These are the very scenes appearing on the tombs which they thus transformed into a moving, complex prayer, a "reading" before God, an objuration to Him to be faithful to His own mercy and law, and to the hopes and love of His children.

It will be readily agreed that all such incidents were full of vitality. The most "spectacular" among them showed the passage of the Jews across the Red Sea as the Egyptian army was swallowed by the waves; the adventures of Jonah; the sacrifice of Isaac; the cured paralytic carrying his cot on his back; and Lazarus rising from the tomb.

All these subjects, despite appearances to the contrary, were without any narrative design: We are dealing with sculptured prayers, not stories. We find no contemporary scenes—especially none showing a martyrdom—and no episodes from the Passion. But little by little, the iconography was enriched. From the Old Testament came Adam and Eve, their temptation and expulsion; the sacrifices of Cain and Abel (but no trace of Abel's murder); Tobias and the ascent of Elias into heaven. And from the New Testament appear, beginning with the fourth century, the Nativity;[12] the Adoration of the Magi, including camels and palm trees; the Marriage at Cana; Jesus and the Samaritan woman conversing at the well; Zachary on his sycamore tree; and Christ's entrance into Jerusalem on Palm Sunday.

Henceforth, funerary art-work would no longer be directed only to God to petition Him on behalf of a dead person; it would also be intended for the living, to teach them about episodes from the "heroic deeds" of God. The scenes depicted would no longer be limited to a kind of timeless evidence of His saving powers but would contain also an account of all He had done for men and, in the person of Christ, of all He had done and suffered among men and for them. The Passion of Christ appeared for the first time in art—Pilate washing his hands; Peter denying the Master (as the cock close by Peter's feet clearly reminds the viewer); Jesus being scourged and carrying His Cross. After the Gospels, there would appear in sculpture scenes from the Acts of the Apostles, including the deeds of St Peter and St Paul.

There was no sign at all, as yet, of the Crucifixion, which was avoided in various ways. In fact, the Crucifixion was, so to speak, completely engrossed by the concept of the Resurrection which, in turn, was evoked abstractly. We find,

[12] In this same period there appeared, either on sarcophagi or on ivories, scenes borrowed from the apocryphal Gospels—a practice widely used during the Middle Ages. These scenes included the ox, donkey and midwife in the stable at Bethlehem; and the angel leading the Holy Family on their flight into Egypt.

for example, on a sarcophagus in the Lateran, the Cross between two sleeping soldiers and scenes of the Passion. But the Cross is bare, decorated at its top only with a monogram encircled by a triumphal crown. Everything was stated, for those who understood the symbolism, but nothing was shown. On the wooden doors of the Church of Santa Sabina, in Rome, Christ is shown standing between the two thieves, who are smaller in size than the Lord. All three figures have their arms open and half-raised, but they are not attached to crosses (in fact, no crosses appear); those "crucified" forms are still *orantes,* or praying figures.

For a long time, the cross of suffering was either avoided or deliberately shown without blood. In evoking the Eucharistic wine, for example, the artists showed the Good Shepherd with a flask over his shoulder, in preference to depicting the condemned Man with the wound in His side. The extraordinary popularity of Christ's monogram, which was to exist across such distance and for so long a time, can apparently be attributed to the fact that this symbol brought together Christ and the Cross, but in a radically stylized and, as it were, algebraic form. Why should Christ be shown in the act of dying and dead since He underwent death only in order to destroy it? [13] The first images of Christ on the Cross appeared in the sixth century on works of ivory.

It is worthwhile to pause for a minute and consider how the early Christians depicted Jesus and His mother, those two essential figures in the iconography yet to come. We find not the slightest evidence of concern with realism—for example, an attempt to suggest a Semitic type. Mary was identified by her position near the crib. If shown by herself, she might be confused with any Roman matron or

[13] Later, as we shall see, people reasoned quite differently, particularly in order to call a halt to Docetism. The history of the Crucifix through the ages is a continuous evolution in the direction of realism.

orante. Jesus was depicted as a beardless youth[14]—sometimes as a boy with round, doll-like features. The same was
true of Daniel, who could be identified only by the lions
that surrounded him (and by his nudity). Suzannah as an
orante differed from the Virgin only in being shown with
the two elders who spied on her. Another figure of Christ,
which was developed a little later, was scarcely less conventional than the type mentioned above: His beard and
draped toga were of Roman rather then Palestinian origin.
But nothing of this sort should surprise us. This was but the
first evidence of a fact confirmed, without exception, by
many different types of iconography. Christian art never
considered presenting a Jesus with "local colour" until the
misguided attempts of some unimportant "archaeological"
artists of the last century. The traditional attitude sprang
from a deep theological intuition, for if God became a Jew,
during the days of Tiberius Caesar, the main point of this
fact was that He became man not for a handful of coreligion-
ists but for all of us, even for men of today. By clothing figures
of the Gospel in togas and tunics, the sculptors of the fourth
century only did what those who came after them would do
when they clothed their figures in armour, tunics, doublets
and farthingales.

*   *   *

From the viewpoint of plastic values, the Hellenistic tradition offered the sculptor an abundant treasure of skills:
the sense of movement, flowing drapery, a rich and varied
composition, "impressionistic" trends. All these can be seen
on the sarcophagi: For example, on the so-called tomb of
St Quiteria at Mas-d'Aire in the Landes region, the volutes
of Jonah's sea monster catch the spectator's eye in their
skilful swirl. Elsewhere a woman is shown holding her nose

[14] Sarcophagus of Junius Bassus, at Rome, about 300.

beside Lazarus who, as the Gospel relates, was "already stinking". And a direct recollection of scenes showing the battles of Alexander the Great passed into reliefs of the defeat of Pharaoh's army. The composition was most varied: At times, it consisted of but a single scene; at other times, it might be divided into several episodes shown side-by-side and somewhat confusedly; again the composition might be divided into separate compartments by little columns or by palm trees. Heavy relief gave emphasis to the modelled forms, but often at the expense of the over-all effect: One's attention was focussed on many different details, and the religious significance was frittered away in scenes of a narrative, quaint, touching or amusing nature, totally lacking in grandeur.

The narrative spirit was in competition with a quite different trend before which it was, in the end, quite to disappear. The new trend was a revival of the Eastern feeling for art. In contrast to the Hellenistic predilection for the human body, the Oriental tradition had a bent towards symmetry, line-patterns and volume, and the "truth" of the depicted subject—if there is one at all—was sacrificed to purely decorative attempts at balance and movement. Technically, this led to a decided fondness, so far as sculpture was concerned, for low, almost flattened relief, in which the designs appeared to be appliquéd or embroidered in the background. This general tendency, which we shall note again later, was particularly noticeable on the sarcophagi because narrative exuberance had been most widely lavished on such art-forms. In Gaul, in addition to the tombs at Arles, which were heavily covered with human figures full of action, the region of Aquitaine produced tombs which spontaneously limited themselves to monograms of Christ, crowns, scroll-patterns, strigils, stars, and animals confronting each other in front of a vase. Émile Mâle associated such a preference with the Visigothic invasion of this region and of Spain at the beginning of the fifth century. The Ostrogoths of Theodoric, on the other hand, seized Italy, and made Ravenna their capital. And the sarcophagi of Ravenna (which date from the fifth and sixth centuries and the first half of the seventh) bore the same decorative motifs, renouncing the human figure for stags or birds, vine-branches, spiral-shaped fringes and monograms of Christ flanked by the Alpha and Omega. They were works of a splendid decorative power, but they showed a rapid recession, from a technical viewpoint, in effects of depth and movement and the narrative variety of their iconography.

It is curious to note that everything helped to bring about this revenge of the East on the Hellenistic tradition. The new trend came from the North, through the Goths who had known Asiatic art along the Black Sea. A little later, it was to come directly from Byzantium when the Eastern emperors reconquered Rome. It was to come from Syria and Egypt across the Mediterranean. It is obvious that, everywhere in the sixth and seventh centuries, the Greco-Roman tradition had disappeared for a long time to come. And with it went the living, direct and fleshy feeling for sculpture. A tomb from Charenton-sur-Cher, now in the Museum of the Berri at Bourges, was decorated with a line drawing of Daniel among lions, griffons and peacocks. The lines—at least those for the animals—are rigidly noble and perfectly balanced in effect. But we are no longer dealing with a piece of sculpture.

CHAPTER II

BYZANTIUM

Not so long ago, the style known as "early Christian art" was limited, more or less, to catacomb paintings and sculpture on sarcophagi. Investigations in the East, however, have called to our attention, especially in Egypt and Syria, important vestiges of monumental sculpture attributed to the period before the Islamic conquest. They have made it possible to measure the debt Rome and Byzantium owed those regions.

In Syria capitals have been found on which the Corinthian acanthus had undergone remarkable changes. The foliage had acquired a certain drier quality; it stood out less and, instead of forming by itself the mass of the capital, it was rather veneered onto the geometric volume to which it was wedded. In place of capitals looking like stylized bushes, many-sided figures with a leaf-like decoration were developed. An artistic effect was sought through a system of two planes: Ornamental networks retained the light against a background of shadow. In addition, geometric or stylized motifs, such as animals, an urn or a cross, were introduced.

Coptic art,[1] for its part, presented rather similar tendencies on the capitals, lintels and archivolts at Bauit and Sakkarah: a very geometric leaf-like decoration, in flattened relief, on

---

[1] The term "Coptic" is used to describe the Christian culture of Egypt from the Edict of Milan in 313 to the Arab Conquest in 640.

plain surfaces. Its decorative repertory preserved the three-centered cross of the Pharaohs, which had been Christianized. Finally, in Tunisia there have been numerous discoveries of plates of moulded terra cotta, showing traces of ancient painting and representing the same subjects or decorative motifs current on the sarcophagi. They were probably used as friezes in the decoration of churches.

The important point is that such art-forms from Syria and Egypt show a falling-off of moulded forms in favour of hollowed-out designs. The sculptured stone has become a flat slab. It has been worked with a chisel or a trepanning instrument for the purpose of creating holes full of shadow. The finest example of this "surface sculpture" can be seen in the Church of Agthamar in Kurdistan, which dates from about 920. Friezes and medallions were gaily scattered around the building to furnish a harmonious composition played by a combination of sun and shadows. The subject —rows of animals, saints, hunting-scenes, vine plants—were only a pretext for an embroidery which was both humble and full of glory, which had no thought at all of being monumental by itself but only—to quote a phrase of Eupalinos—of "causing the monument to sing without becoming talkative".

Of course, it is wrong to say that Byzantium had no sculpture, but there is a large element of truth in such a statement. In order to grasp this concept more firmly and discover its shades of meaning, we should explore the chronological—and theological—aspects of the question. Early Byzantine art—that is, art before the time of Justinian —had its main centers at Antioch, which was destroyed by the Avars in 562, and at Alexandria. The latter city remained a great center of learning, commerce and art; and Egypt, where eremitism and cenobitism began, had a considerable influence in the Christian world. As we have already seen, the porphyry tombs were of Egyptian origin. So also were the sculptured friezes or panels of cedar wood, traces of which have been found. Art-work on bones and ivory also came from Egypt. This was the case for the famous Trivulce ivory, and other similar works, still very Hellenistic in feeling and showing picturesque scenes (for example, the soldiers sleeping around the rotunda of the Holy Sepulchre; the Holy Women of Jerusalem greeted by a wingless angel; a beardless Christ rising to heaven after the Resurrection) and also figures draped in light and airy fashion, such as the angel in London's British Museum. The throne of Bishop Maximian at Ravenna, which dates from the sixth century, might be attributed to either Antioch or Alexandria (the inclusion of the story of Joseph in Egypt would make us think rather of the latter city).

During the reign of Justinian, however, Constantinople clearly became the main artistic center. Sculpture had its own role to play, chiefly in two areas: the interior decoration of churches, and works in ivory. (Statuary in the round had practically disappeared by this time.) The sanctuaries required sculpture for capitals and imposts; the most beautiful examples can still be seen at San Vitale in Ravenna, Santa Sophia in Constantinople, and—until its destruction— could be seen at St Demetrius in Salonika. The material used was marble, which came mainly from the quarries of Proconesis. The Corinthian style was modified in the same way as for the Syrian and Coptic works we have already described. The abacuses were decorated with animals placed face to face.

The same tendencies, applied in a different way, might be observed on works replying to completely new needs of a specifically Christian nature: the decoration of *ciboria*— types of baldachins, or raised canopies, above the altars— which might also be adorned by the goldsmith's work; pulpits, or platforms, on which clerics stood to read the Epistle and the Gospel to the faithful; chancels, or the enclosed part of the choir; and grill-works, intended to protect the "confessions" where the relics of saints were kept. Chancels and grill-works were partitions, and the latter were always open-worked, but *ciboria* and pulpits were conceived as surfaces for decoration, and each of them presented unique opportunities for developing austere splendours of geometric ornamentation (monograms, crosses, stars, spirals); for ornamentations based on plant-life (boughs, stems, flower-work); and for ornamentation inspired by animals (lions, griffons, eagles, stags and peacocks). It should be further noted that these three categories—the human figure has been totally banished—were closely mingled not only because they were placed side by side on the same field of ornamentation but also because they were combined. Wreaths and vines, slashed leaves, feathers, aigrettes and tails were woven into interlocking compositions with no other law than that of arabesques to be displayed and balanced.

Ivories were the other flourishing form of Byzantine sculpture. A great many of these works have been preserved in churches and museums, a phenomenon explained by the volume of their production and the ease of their transport. The beauty of the material and its workmanship soon induced Christians to make use of carved ivory plaques as covers for copies of the Gospels and also as pyxes.[2]

As was the case with sarcophagi, some pagan ivories were used again. Moreover, when the iconography of the ivories was Christianized, it was closely related to that found on the tombs, as can be easily deduced from such examples as the Trivulce ivory, the reliquary at Brescia, the throne of Maximian and the ivory from Saint-Lupicin now in the Bibliothèque Nationale.

Thanks to ivories like these, certain themes—such as Christ on the Cross, and the Madonna and Child, which were destined to have a dazzling success in later times—

[2] Round boxes in which hosts are kept.

were first introduced to Christendom. The Christian iconography and the ornamental repertory of the East were
carried to distant nations principally in the form of ivories.
By enlarging those ivories clumsily in stone, the West was
able to keep alive something of the great tradition of decoration in relief, and thus the art of sculpture itself could
be reborn little by little—without having to begin again
solely from the art of the goldsmith or from two-dimensional
models derived separately from miniatures and fabrics.

*   *   *

Now is the time to trace the main facts in the long, cruel
controversy over the iconoclasts, or image-breakers, a factor
which for more than a century—from 726 to 843—over-
shadowed Byzantine art. The treatment we must give to
sculpture is not easily fixed, since the word "images" had
a very general meaning. Even though the debate had to do
especially with figures in paintings or mosaics, which were
so obvious in the churches, there was all the more reason,
as we have seen, why carved statues, too, might cause
scandal. The law of Moses and the law of Christ and the
Apostles were invoked, then, in the very heart of Christendom against an internal danger of idolatrous corruption.[3]

From the fourth century on, there were indications of
hostility toward images. Later, rioting broke out, apparently
under Jewish instigation, in connection with a wave of propaganda from Asia Minor. As a matter of fact, the reverence
shown to images had taken on highly suspect aspects: They
were regarded somewhat like living persons endowed with
supernatural power; children received them in baptism as
their god-fathers or god-mothers; bits of them were removed
and eaten, for were not Christ and the saints materially
present in them as in another form of the Eucharist? Popu-

[3] Cf. Deut. 4: 15–19; Acts 17: 29: etc.

lar factions rioted for or against the holy images, just as they did over the horse-races in the circus.

Despite a distinct inclination towards the abstract in sculpture, Byzantium also continued to carve figures and scenes. Quite apart from the carved ivories, we know that Santa Sophia, at the time of Justinian, had capitals showing scenes from the life of Christ and our Lady, as well as angels, prophets and saints. The council known as the Quinisext, which was held in 692, took a position against allegorical art in order to put a stop to Docetism:[4] "We order that, in place of the lamb of ancient times, there should be shown the Lamb who has taken away the sins of the world, Christ our God, in human form."

In 726, a violent reaction against images was officially initiated by an edict of Leo the Isaurian. An officer sent to destroy an image of Christ in the imperial palace was killed in a scuffle. In 753, the Council of Hieria[5] drew up a systematic program of image-breaking. It decreed that every image is, by necessity, heretical, since the divine nature of Christ cannot be shown in a material way. The Host is the only possible "image" of the Saviour, but the Cross still was entitled to respect, provided it was shown *without a figure*.[6] Even the sanctuaries in the rocks of Cappadocia, whence every image was banished, had great carved crosses on the ceilings. During the reign of the Empress Irene, the Second Council of Nicea, in 787, restored the images, stating: Did not Christ take on flesh "to deliver us from the wickedness of the idolaters"? Did not the angels appear to the righteous under human form? Were the prophets and saints bodiless? "Their images, by recalling to us the originals, might lead us to some form of participation in their

[4] The Docetist heresy taught that the Word only appeared to assume a human nature.

[5] This council, like the Quinisext, was not recognised by the Holy See.

[6] Cf. Gal. 6: 14.

holiness. People may kiss them and bow down before them.
. . . But this is a relative kind of devotion: We shall reserve
to God alone what is properly called worship, as well as
our faith".

Under Leo the Armenian, in 815, iconoclasm flared up
once more, and again during the reign of Theophilus (829–
842) whose widow Theodora definitively re-established respect for images in 843.

One of the results of the iconoclastic movement—surprising at first glance but logical—was the return to favour of
profane, even pagan, subjects in art; for example, ivory
boxes decorated with scenes of hunting, war, horse-races
and mythological legends. The opponents of the images were
not Puritans demanding an out-and-out austerity. Profane
subjects were matters of indifference to them, and might even
be well regarded; what they persecuted were the "holy"
images which, by reason of their subject-matter, were considered blasphemous.

In fact, the struggle was a confusing one,[7] and we find
false partisanship and sound views on both sides. The popes
expressed vigorous opposition to the iconoclastic heresy.
But the West also became involved in the controversy
through the Caroline Books, which were written at the behest
of Charlemagne. This work took a stand against contradictory councils of both 753 and 787, and in particular against
the decrees of Nicea which, moreover, were only known to
the author of the Caroline Books through a poor Latin translation. Its arguments tended to denounce idolatry by both
sides: The worship of images means paying too much honour
to them, and is a scandal. But breaking images is also a
scandal and means paying them too much honour. For in a

[7] St John of Damascus, a Syrian employed by the Moslem caliphs
of Damascus, was an ardent defender of the images, despite the
fact that he had many reasons for becoming "Islamicized".

certain way such conduct indicates *belief* in the images[8] and grants them a particular effect which they do not have at all. Worship belongs only to God, reverence belongs only to the saints, and to their images belongs a respect which does not in any way commit the soul. How many burning debates of the spirit—debates which were to be constantly born again throughout history—might have been exorcised by that wise statement of long ago!

*   *   *

Quite obviously, the controversy over the images during the seventh and eighth centuries only accentuated the trends already noted in the development of decoration. As a result, the artistic flowering known as the Second Golden Age produced in Italy at such centers as Ravenna, St Mark's in Venice, Torcello and Ancona, and in Greece at the Monastery of St Luke and the Little Metropolitan Church of Athens some chancels and panels similar to sixth-century works.

The art of statuary was regarded at Byzantium with particular suspicion long before the iconoclastic crisis, and this suspicion has continued. Up to our own time, in fact, sculpture in the round has been forbidden in the religious art of the East. Figures in bas-relief, however, have been adopted; for example, in the decoration of the iconostases. The most beautiful surviving work of this kind is in Santa Maria in Porto at Ravenna. It represents, in marble, the Virgin Mary as an *orante* (the most frequent subject for such pieces). The figure is dignified and gentle, and the chaste folds of Mary's veil and gown are decorated with hollowed-out crosses.

In addition, statuettes in high relief were used in the

[8] Cf. on this point, an accurate survey by L. Réau in *Monuments détruits de l'art français*, Vol. I, p. 18.

decoration of archivolts. Toward the end of this period, a certain renaissance of sculpture was observed, marking a rebound of Western influence. Thus we note a thirteenth-century bas-relief of Adam and Eve at Trebizond and the wooden doors of St Nicholas of Ochrida, which were certainly inspired by a similar work in Italy. Both, in turn, were more or less directly inspired by the art of the bronze-workers at Constantinople. Thus we have completed the circle back again to works of metal and ivory.

The six great figures of women executed in stucco[9] at Cividale in the Friuli region of Italy, about which so much has been written, and the figures on the *ciborium* of Sant' Ambrogio at Milan—no matter what their exact date of composition may be—were all rejoinders, executed in a cheap, easy-to-work material and on a grandiose style, of models carried out in some precious material. And the bronze plaques of this period were but "translations" of ivories. For man's plastic sense and love of noble figures found expression in ivories as well as in gold and hammered silver.[10]

Such works took the form of panels of relief sculpture; they might be panels of a single fold, triptychs or polyptichs. The figures included Christ in majesty surrounded by His Mother and John the Baptist,[11] and at the sides or bottom of the panel were shown such "high officials" of the heavenly court as the archangels and saints.[12] Other subjects included the Madonna and Child; Christ placing crowns on the heads of the emperor and empress; the stories of Joseph (as in

[9] Stucco decorations were frequent up to the eleventh century; for example, at the abbeys of Saint-Riquier, of Saint-Rémi in Reims, and of Mals in the Tirol. But few have survived.

[10] Cf. Syrian silverwork of the fourth to the sixth centuries (the chalice of Antioch and the plates of Kerynia).

[11] This arrangement, known as the *deisis,* shows Mary and John the Baptist interceding before Christ as Judge.

[12] Especially favoured are the *stratilates,* or warrior saints, such as George, Theodore and Eustace.

the Treasury at Sens) or of David; and the twelve great
feasts of the Church from the Annunciation to the Coronation of our Lady. The postures, movements, faces and
draperies display a noble, graceful elegance; a true religious
grandeur is manifested in those small art objects.

Such was the priceless legacy which Byzantium left to
the future art of sculpture. It was not executed in stone,
but the stone carvers of the West were to receive it—at
times awkwardly and slavishly, and at other times freely and
gloriously. For Christian sculpture had died, once and for
all time, in the East.

CHAPTER III

THE DARK AGES

Monumental sculpture in stone did not appear again until about the year 1000. For the Carolingian renaissance, which was in any case ephemeral, was not concerned with this art-form. It should not be thought, however, that there was no sculpture at all. A marked decline in technique took place, especially after the Arab invasion destroyed the marble-workers' studios in the Pyrenees.[1] In addition, there was hostility or reticence on the part of the clergy, who were often ready—like a certain Flodoard in the tenth century—to fear such statues might shelter a remnant of paganism. Both these factors more or less extinguished, though they did not absolutely kill, the nostalgia or desire for stone images.

First of all, monumental sculpture was very much alive during the seventh and eighth centuries in two regions on the western-most edge of Europe: in Visigothic Spain, and in Ireland and Northumbria. The first region has left us, at Tarrasa and elsewhere, capitals derived from the Corinthian acanthus, simplified and treated in a "geometric" fashion. This region is especially known, however, for its decorated panels with their splendid mongrams of Christ.[2]

Ireland's outdoor steles and crosses of carved stone are most curious. This form of decoration is a direct continua-

---

[1] For Charlemagne's own tomb a Roman sarcophagus was re-used.
[2] This subject, or symbol, stayed in favour for a long time in Spain and in the Pyrenees region for the decoration of tympanums.

tion of the pagan art of the Iron Age: The cross is shown
with all the motifs dear to makers of barbaric jewellery—
spirals, swastikas, roses, braids, interlocking figuers as well
as animals transformed into four-footed creepers or feroci-
ous-looking designs. If human figures are shown, they represent a tangle of Celtic myths and legends vaguely adapted
to Christianity; we cannot be sure that this or that scene of
warfare really is meant to depict the exploits of Joshua or
Gideon.

Themes of indisputably Christian origin came to those
distant lands from Egypt. There is no doubt about the
existence of contacts between those two countries endowed
with monasticism—especially after the Coptic monks were
forced to flee the Arab invasion. Beginning with the late
seventh century, we find representations of Christ on the
Cross, wearing a long robe; David as a harpist or warrior;
Jonah; David among the lions; SS Antony and Paul the
Hermit sharing a piece of bread; and Jacob wrestling with
the angel. The last three themes gave the artist an opportunity to display interlocking or face-to-face designs that can
be traced to far-off Asia.

Later, during the ninth and early tenth centuries, the
crosses were decorated with a dogmatic *Summa*: the Old
Testament was on one side and the New Testament on the
other; the Crucifixion, as a symbol of the Redemption, was
in the center and the Last Judgement on the reverse side.
Beginning with the eleventh century—under the impact of
the Norse invasions—the powerful originality of those monuments yielded to foreign influences, and the remarkable
artistic autonomy of Ireland and Northumbria was eclipsed.[3]

[3] There is no doubt that a certain recollection of the "spirit" of
those island crosses was rediscovered much later in the calvaries of
Brittany. But since the calvaries do not antedate the sixteenth century, they obviously had a completely different iconographic and
technical heritage. The stone slab, however, on which can be made
out the Fall of Man and the Last Judgement, at Tonoën, reminds

That sculpture stirs us because one can see growing there, under the strong winds of the Atlantic, a wild shoot of Christian sculpture whose seed was brought from far away. In their crude awkwardness, those island stone-cutters preserved as well as they could—certainly better than their contemporaries on the European continent—the qualities of monumentality and volume.

The best way to show what happened to stone sculpture elsewhere between the seventh and eleventh centuries is to choose several works which mark its course.

At Venasque in 605, the lid to Bishop Boethius' tomb was fashioned. It is a slab adorned with a large cross containing the Alpha and Omega, two six-spoked wheels and two six-pointed stars—all in very low relief. In addition, there are two small hollowed-out crosses. On the cross and the bands separating the different motifs we find hollowed-out sockets which formerly were encrusted with coloured stones. This monument represents the enlargement and transformation of a *staurothèque*.[4]

A number of works of sculpture, including the lintel of Saint-Genis-des-Fontaines (erected in 1020) and the cross at Arles-sur-Tech are mere "translations" into stone of pieces of jewellery originally imported and later produced locally in the studios of artists who have left us many masterpieces in the form of reliquaries, chalices, bindings of the Gospels and altar-panels.

In such cases it is clear that the craftsman's point of departure is a flat surface. He can only disengage, on a field shaped like a shallow basin, a jutting surface itself flat, and the details are indicated schematically by line engraving. The techniques employed are those of cutting, punching,

---

one indeed of the island stones. The so-called Celtic crosses of Brittany, which are hard to date, are clipped monoliths, without any decorative carvings.

[4] A reliquary intended to house a piece of the "true cross".

grooving, incision and inlay. The purpose of all such opera-
tions is to start with a flat surface and treat it in such a
way as to achieve relief as a form of decoration. In true
sculpture, however, the surfaces and planes respect in their
"movements" the dominance of the relief forms to which
they are wedded.[5]

A critical comment is perhaps appropriate here concerning such works, for it is stylish today to go into ecstasy over
them. The Dark Ages are expected to give us an illumination peculiar only to that period of history—a sense of
plastic values stripped of servitude to physical resemblance
and narrative skill. Indeed, we are supposed to see a kind of
spirituality all the more profound for being obscure, all the
more ineffable because we cannot find in it—for good reasons—any consistency.

This shows a curious evolution of artistic taste. During
the nineteenth century, as people began to admire mediaeval
art, they first adopted a pathos-ridden, sloppy kind of
Middle Ages—the fifteenth century of Victor Hugo. Then
they went back to the glories of the thirteenth century. Only
later did they pay proper credit to the twelfth century as
the period that had produced, in its turn, masterpieces of
Christian sculpture. Ardent researchers like Puig y Cafadalch
and great aesthetes like Focillon went back to the origins in
their valuable studies. Unfortunately, they opened the way,
despite themselves, to a horde of avant-garde followers who
—unless care be taken—will in the end obscure the facts and
throw away common-sense. Under the pretext that, a hun-

[5] This statement is applicable, for example, to the two martyrs
bound to a cross in the hypogeum, or cellar, at Mellebaude near
Poitiers (seventh century); to the Crucifixion at Saint-Mesme de
Chinon (tenth century); to the capitals at Cruas; and also to
numerous stones carved in low relief which are found, either separately or as part of a frieze, in the walls at Saint-Benoit-sur-Loire,
La Celle-Bruère, Chabris, Saint-Restitut, Saint-Paul-Trois-Châteaux,
etc. The last-named works appear to date from the tenth and eleventh
centuries.

dred years ago, many characteristics of Romanesque art
were interpreted as "clumsiness", whereas we see in them
today proofs of genius and skill, such critics no longer wish
to recognize any clumsiness in them at all. It is clear, however, that the artisans of that period only did as well as they
could, at a time when every technical tradition for giving
life to stone had been lost. The critics will never cease examining those flat, misshapen gnomes, those animal and human forms which are only aberrant in their own defense.
Such works are touching, exciting, even upsetting—but they
are not beautiful. They are valuable, just as nuts and roots
are infinitely valuable in time of famine.

To sum up, those works are substitutes for sculpture.
The stone the artisans used betrayed them, and the artisans
themselves betrayed the stone. By transposing into stone
what they had admired in gold, silver, ivory or cloth, the
men of that period failed to respect the requirements and
skills peculiar to their materials. Because of their own in-
ability, they cheated on what they had a right to "expect"
from stone. What is it that makes a world of difference between the well-known high-relief carvings in the choir of St
Sernin at Toulouse and the Christ and angels at Moissac?
The pieces at Toulouse are simply ivories, executed in
marble and enlarged fifty or a hundred times, while the
work at Moissac is truly of stone—the same stone used to
build God's house which has now learned how to look up to
heaven and sing His glory in its own tongue. On one hand
we are dealing with an art of imitation fixed by its own dryness at the base of a wall; by contrast, Moissac offers us the
triumphal door-way of man's resurrection.

Another landmark is the crypt at Jouarre, a building of
the late seventh century which wins our admiration on many
counts. Its capitals of Pyrenean marble have an elegance
whose secret has been lost. The sarcophagi of two abbesses
—Theodechilda and Aguilberta—are impressively harmoni-

ous. This is particularly the case for Theodechilda's tomb, on which are found rows of sea-shells (or perhaps round leaves with radiating veins) forming a network of curved lozenges. Another monument at Jouarre—the tomb of Agilbert—seems astonishingly ahead of its period. Christ in majesty (although still beardless) is shown among the four symbols of the Evangelists. On one side of the tomb is a scene of the resurrection of the elect, who crowd about their Judge and raise their arms in jubilation. This work, far more than the two sarcophagi just mentioned, conveys a sense of movement that makes us think of the great tympanums created four centuries later. Our favorable judgement is maintained in spite of the awkward treatment of the surface space, which was cut out obliquely in order to leave more space on one side than the other.

In all the art-forms associated with stone—tombs, the decoration of walls and partitions, and capitals—sculpture between the seventh and eleventh centuries was a poor kind of art which only survived by copying other arts and by hesitating procedures. We must look to quite different media —for example, metal work—to find the great artists of that period, men who showed a sense of vigourous form and strongly articulated, well-balanced volume.

* * *

The art of bronze-casting was practiced at Constantinople, and in 838, Santa Sophia was adorned with bronze doors. The studios of Constantinople continued to flourish, and unquestionably produced the portals of Amalfi (1076), St Paul's-Outside-the-Walls at Rome, and Salerno.[6] Later, doors of this type were also made in Italy itself.[7]

[6] Those works were composed of rectangular panels about 16″ by 20″ in size, which could be easily exported. They were assembled on the spot.

[7] At Troja, Trani, Ravello, Monreale, Benevento and Pisa (twelfth century).

Elsewhere, during the reign of Charlemagne, Aix-la-Chapelle became an important center of bronze-work. The Emperor adorned his palace chapel with a large door and three small portals. A lion's muzzle has a vigour of modelling which was not surpassed by any similar work cast in the twelfth century.

Germany continued to be a major center of bronze-casting. Two centuries later, about 1020, Archbishop Bernard of Hildesheim commissioned sixteen panels for the portal of his cathedral as well as a column decorated with spirals. The studios at Magdeburg exported bronze-works all over Europe—for example, to San Zeno in Verona, to Gniezno in Poland and as far as Novgorod in Russia (1152–1156). In all that production, the decoration at first consisted mainly of crosses, monograms and motifs of a purely ornamental nature. Human figures were rare at first, but became more frequent later as door panels were filled with picturesque scenes taken from the Old and New Testaments. The laws of perspective were cheerfully disregarded; effects of gradation in light and shadow and depth (in which an artist like Ghiberti was to excel one day) were unknown; and the figures, at times, could be included only at the price of ridiculous distortions and acrobatics. They appeared stamped out against a smooth background. Their heads, however, often deliberately jutted out and were, indeed, in the round; this treatment of the heads caused the volume of the figures to stand out freely although the bodies remained in the background.

In the tenth century, a striking innovation took place—statues of precious metals. The goldsmith's or silversmith's art had continued to produce works of outstanding quality. The barbarians, while unused to any tradition of monumental sculpture, excelled in metal-working, and their preferences and ability soon found in western Europe a kind of alliance with similar trends from Byzantium. Although a

very great many works have been lost, numerous examples
have survived. The goldsmiths sometimes worked in an
almost monumental style, constructing images of saints in
high relief beneath blind arcades. This is the form of the
famous golden frontal of the Basel altar,[8] which depicts, in
the center, a figure of Christ, standing and blessing the
donors who are shown crouched at His feet. To Christ's
right are St Michael the Archangel and St Benedict; to
His left are the archangels Gabriel and Raphael. It is a
work of the highest beauty—flexible, majestic and serene.
Despite its costly materials, the frontal is wonderfully modest
in feeling and is, in the purest sense of the word, a "classic".

On the other hand, the figure-reliquaries are works of
sculpture in the round. In 946, Bishop Stephen of Clermont,
in the Auvergne, commissioned one of his clerics, Aleaume
(who was also an architect, goldsmith and sculptor), to
make a statue of "our Lady in majesty" from wood sheathed
in gold and encrusted with precious stones. In 980, another
work of this type was reported at Ely in England. A third
work of the same date has been preserved at Essen in the
Rhineland.[9] Mary is of gold and has enamel eyes. The apple
in her hand—the symbol of the new Eve—is a filigree encrusted with precious stones; the Child's halo is of the same
materials. France has a famous statue of St Foy at Conques,
and at one time there were many other statues of this type,
especially in the Auvergne.[10]

[8] Completed apparently about 1020 at Fulda, this work was donated
to the cathedral of Basel by the Emperor Henry II. Walled up during the sixteenth century to save it from iconoclasts and robbers, it
is now in the Cluny museum in Paris. It is about 39″ by 68½″ in
size.

[9] It appears that this is the most ancient surviving *statue* of our
Lady.

[10] The "Majesties" of St Géraud at Aurillac and St Martial at
Limoges no longer exist. But the statues of St Baudime at Saint-
Nectaire and of St Césaire at Maurs, both dating from the twelfth
century, can be directly traced to pre-Romanesque works.

Such works enjoyed enormous fame, which is easily explained. The life-sized figures, sparkling with jewels and gold in the flickering candlelight, exercised a kind of fascination on the spectator. Even today, he feels transfixed by their enamel glance fixed on infinity. And thus we see reappear, in relation to these figures, the same feelings that caused at Byzantium the quarrel over the images. According to the legend, Gerbert, the Pope from the Auvergne, built a head of gilded brass which would answer questions put to it—a fable obviously based on statues of the kind we have been discussing. In such instances, was not the image regarded as the saint himself come down from heaven, his glorious body clothed for all eternity? On the other hand, could it not be considered an idol? Early in the eleventh century, the theologian Bernard, while on a pilgrimage to Aurillac, poked fun at this situation. But he also became angry over it until the miraculous intervention of St Foy herself brought about his repentance.[11]

We are dealing here with great works of sculpture, as can be confirmed by the statue of our Lady of Paderborn, which dates from about 1060. In the seventeenth century, its golden

[11] Here, as transcribed by André Michel, is an interesting passage on this matter: "In the whole region of the Auvergne, the Rouergue and nearby areas, every church has erected to the saint it venerates a statue made of gold, silver or some other metal, which contains in a dignified way either the head of the saint or some other relic . . . When I saw on the altar the statue of St Geraud, so similar in appearance to a human figure that the peasants believed they could discern in the brilliance of the saint's glance the fulfillment of their prayers, I turned to my companion Bernier and said to him in Latin, with an ironic smile: 'What do you think about this idol? Would not Jupiter or Mars have been pleased with such a statue?' In truth, it seems unsuitable and absurd to shape an image of wood, plaster or bronze, except for the figure of the Saviour on the Cross . . . As for the saints, they should be shown to our eyes only through lifelike descriptions in books or wall paintings . . . But that abuse has become so prevalent in those regions that, if I had spoken aloud, I should doubtless have received the punishments reserved for major criminals.

clothing was stripped away and melted down. What was left is the statue's core, or "soul", a piece of linden-wood. But truly that *is* the statue's soul. For the Virgin in majesty, with the Child on her knees, is shown in an attitude of benediction, and she has remained beautiful—with a pure, dignified and virgin beauty.[12]

Those works clearly attracted so much energetic admiration and piety on the part of the faithful that they became —for the first time in the West—examples of a fixed type of image. This factor accounts for some unexpected archaisms.[13] In many regions, especially in the Auvergne and Catalonia, painted wooden statues of the Virgin in majesty were produced during the twelfth century. Mary was shown seated on a magnificent chair, her feet carefully resting on the ground. Beneath the long, stiff folds of her veil, the Virgin's inexpressive face has wide-open eyes. The Child sits on His Mother's lap, also looking straight at the worshipper. With the exception of Jesus' hand, which is raised in benediction, the group obeys a law of strict frontality. A relic container is hollowed out in the back of the group. This model was so well received that similar statues were still being carved in the fourteenth century and even much later.[14] They were

---

[12] Is this not, indeed, the characteristic fact about masterpieces of sculpture that their beauty survives mutilation? Are there not many examples of this from the Parthenon to the cathedral of Strasbourg, including a certain statue of Venus worn as smooth as a pebble during the sixteen centuries it was in the sea?

[13] The best-known example is the *Santo Volto* (Holy Countenance) of Lucca—a statue of Christ on the Cross, wearing a long robe, which was still being copied in Britanny during the sixteenth century. But there are many other examples, including the "bon Dieu at Giblot", which was thought to be miraculous in the seventeenth century and was copied many times. The original, a "Christ seated at Calvary", dates from the sixteenth century.

[14] The great stone statue of the Virgin on the south tympanum of the Royal Portal at Chartres, and the statue of the Virgin on the tympanum of Saint Anne's Door at Paris, both of which were carved between 1145 and 1175, are of this same type.

true copies, because popular devotion would not tolerate any other kind of image.

In tracing the direct sculptural influence of St Foy of Conques, we have gone far beyond the "miracle" that gave rise, between 1100 and 1130, to the splendid, monumental sculpture of the Romanesque. We must now turn our attention to this style.

CHAPTER IV

THE ROMANESQUE
PERIOD

Before the year 1118, Renier of Huy cast in bronze a vessel decorated with various scenes we can still admire in the church of St Bartholomew at Liège. Everything shows the hand of a master: the trees with their characteristic foliage, the bodies of water with their gentle waves, and especially the human figures whose faces and gestures modestly suggest something quite new—inner feelings. The surprise we feel before this work reflects our amazement at the sudden radiation of the full-grown Romanesque style. The men of those days were fully aware of the dazzling aspects of their achievement. We can read at the base of a twelfth-century tympanum in Dijon the following proud boast: "Formerly I was coarsely made. Peter gave me the splendour you behold, transforming my earlier crudeness into this more attractive form."

We should keep in mind, first of all, that the development of sculpture during the twelfth century took place in close association with the development of architecture.

Countless church buildings were undertaken in a new, bold and noble style, which summoned the sculptors to take up themes monumental in themselves and quite new: The portal, or monumental entrance to the house of God, was the gathering-place of the faithful. In conjunction with the

portal and above its lintel was the tympanum which proclaimed triumphantly an apocalyptic vision of the entrance
of time into eternity. On either side, the concentric *voussures,*
or grooves, expanded the effect of the central scene, displayed it more fully to us, and summoned our eyes to converge on this scene and on our King. At either side of the
doors, the splayed porch had the double task of radiating to
the world and of inviting the world into the sanctuary. At
this point were placed the statues of the precursors and
propagandists of the Faith: Christ's earthly ancestors, the
kings of the Old Covenant, the prophets and apostles, all
those who lead us to Christ or whom He has delegated for
our sake. The porch of the church took on even more dignity
and powers of attraction if preceded, as at Vézelay, by a
narthex, an area which had both open and covered areas and
offered additional possibilities for decoration.

The sculpture, however, was never something merely
added. Whether the stone was carved in a nearby workshop
before being set into place on the church building, or
whether it was first mounted on the church and then carved
from a scaffolding, it was closely subordinate in function.
The surface of the tympanum has become a bas-relief, but
it still remained a wall. The lintel was covered with roses or
narrative details, but it remained a beam. A rich decoration
clung to the archivolts, but they remained a framework. At
times, a column became a statue, but it was still a column,
scarcely interrupted by the slight edge on which the figure
might lean its feet almost vertically, in a purely architectural
equilibrium, as if levitating in space.

Later sculpture was to become more and more autonomous
with respect to architecture. During the thirteenth century,
however, this law of subordination, although mitigated, was
not taken lightly. When great sculpture was born, it managed
to express, like a handmaiden, a sovereign beauty. Quite apart
from its subject matter, Christian sculpture gave a spiritual

lesson of this beauty in accord with St Thomas Aquinas'
concept when he praised the virtue of *docilitas,* or Bossuet's
concept when he described discipline as more liberating than
revolution or anarchy.

The capital was another area favored by Romanesque
sculpture. The aesthetics of Byzantine art tended to reduce
the capital to a play of surfaces. Now it became again a
thing of volume. The responsibility given to the capital by
an architect was one of transition: normally a transition from
a curve to a straight line, from a vault or arch to a column,
pier or pilaster. In the twelfth century, before the daring
achievements of the Gothic style, a stone faithfully retained
its own weight, and the capital was there to indicate this
fact. Although from the eleventh century on, some capitals
can be found which the sculptor had chipped down for the
sole purpose of decorating the walls, increasingly the capital
was worked in its very volume, and the decorative figure became the capital, instead of just covering it as decoration.
We are no longer faced with a monotonous accumulation of
the old-style acanthus leaves, but find instead extraordinarily
inventive forms consisting of leaves, animals and human
figures which merge with one another and become detached
and then are intertwined; they soar, devour each other and
comingle. The capital was made to be seen from different
angles, to draw the spectator's attention to a particular surface or angle. And from that time on, the artist distributed
the symmetries, accentuated lines and volume towards either
the corners or the center of the surfaces, with a powerful feeling for the effects created by a volume in three dimensions
that has been worked in fulness and symmetry. The capitals
have a solidarity among themselves: They scan the development of the architectural corbel separating the choir from
the ambulatory behind it. In the cloisters, between the light
and shadow, they strike accents on the strings of columns
along the four walks and on the borders of the central open

space. And the capitals create always a feeling of joy and great peace, which springs directly from the eye to the soul; there is no need to stop and ask what they represent. Without those carved monsters and outbursts of imagination, without those phantasmagorias, the sanctuary—paradoxical as it may seem!—would have been less holy and even the *campo santo,* or cemetery, would have been more worldly.

When we speak here of a monumental quality, let us be clear about our meaning. Such sculpture never constituted a monument by itself. Only much later did artists have such an aim in mind. In the twelfth century, it was truly the wall, the column, the capital or the archivolt that raised its voice in song, each in its own order and place. Not one of them sought to draw attention to itself. They were part and parcel of the building. True free-standing sculpture did not yet exist. Even though, during the thirteenth century, the statues were to be completely detached from their background, their bases and canopies were engaged in the mass of the building and remained parts of the wall.[1] In the twelfth century, absolute primacy was given to the law of a statue's position in the ensemble—and this was true even for sculpture in wood.

In connection with this general rule, Focillon pointed out several important aspects of Romanesque sculpture, in particular, what he called "the law of adherence to the cadre, or framework": The artist tends to establish the most points of contact possible between the subject matter and the limits of the space imparted to it. This is the secret of that plenitude

[1] Italy was the first place where free-standing statues were carved in imitation of classical examples. Such statues might be, indeed, of a highly monumental quality, but their effect was quite different. Instead of being subordinated to an architectural complex, such statues had at their disposition—for example, in the middle of a square—the effects of perspective created by an architect. The first example, in France, of a statue carved with equal care on all sides was apparently the statue of St John the Baptist at Rouvres-en-Plaine in the Côte-d'Or district; it dates from the end of the fourteenth century.

which achieves motion without ever losing unity or cohesion, which is abundant without overflowing, which stretches its limbs without becoming spindly.

We are reminded of a statement of Joubert, which, although said in connection with an entirely different situation, may be admirably applied here: "A legitimate authority is one which is aware of its scope and its limitations." The authority of Romanesque sculpture shines in the fact that it fulfills its function regally and at the same time observes its limitations loyally. There are no more gripping examples of this than the panels between the windows at Moissac and Souillac, with their tumultuous and symmetrical hordes of beasts which are both violently released and at the same time still bound according to a strict precalculation. There had been the Greek sense of balance, as represented by the harmonious figures in procession along the Parthenon's frieze. There had been the convulsive fury of barbaric ornamental art. And it is easy to discover traces or analogies of each of them in the masterpieces of French Romanesque sculpture. But what belongs perhaps to this Romanesque art alone is its gift of uniting all the powers of disorder to all the virtues of order, without destroying or harming either.[2]

*   *   *

That order was not just of a plastic nature; it was also theological. We know that high officials of the Church—bishops, abbots and church teachers—were in charge of programs of edification. And that term should be interpreted in its double meaning of building and instructing. Suger and the great abbots of Cluny were outstanding in-

[2] This talent is also typical of the finest Khmer sculpture. Nevertheless, there are certain striking comparisons between the two styles. For example, a certain bas-relief of a lithely dancing female figure with raised arms, which is now in the museum at Cambrai, cannot help but make the spectator think of the *devatas* of Angkor Wat.

tellectual directors of such artistic projects. All were in agreement not to leave to the stone-cutters the task of arranging
decorations according to their own desires. As decreed by the
Council of Nicea, the Church and the official guardians of
her traditions and authority had the responsibility of estab-
lishing a program for artists.[3]

The general effect of such compositions, far from reflecting
the disordered spontaneity incorrectly attributed to them,
was planned to reply to a two-fold yet simple desire: to praise
God's glory and enlighten the minds and souls of men. The
tympanums presented the vision of Ezechiel in all its awful
splendour: the divine Majesty surrounded by the four creatures.[4] Combined with them was St John's vision of the
Apocalypse, including the twenty-four elders. Later a different, but not less grandiose subject matter was to be sub-
stituted: the Last Judgement with angels blowing trumpets,
the resurrection of the dead, and the assignment of souls to
either heaven or hell by decision of the Supreme Judge and
by direction of St Michael the Archangel.

The cloister at Tudela, in Spanish Navarre disclosed,
chapter by chapter, the whole Gospel story, from the Nativity
to the meeting at Emmaus, Pentecost, the conversion of St
Paul, the death of our Lady and her Assumption, the martyr-
doms of SS Andrew and Laurence, St Martin of Tours
sharing his cloak with the beggar, and the removal of St
James's body to Compostella. Even the Old Testament is
represented, through Daniel. The compositions at Moissac
are of equal richness.

Also at Tudela can be deciphered hunting scenes of a hare,

[3] A charming bas-relief in the cloister of the cathedral at Gerona
in Catalonia depicts some sculptors at work in the presence of a
bishop who is not only blessing their task but is also their fore-
man!

[4] The four winged "beings" represent a man, an eagle, a lion and
an ox; soon they were taken as symbols of the four Evangelists,
Matthew, Mark, Luke and John.

a bear and unicorns. At Moissac, scenes of griffons, birds, strange four-footed animals among foliage apparently straight out of a dream or nightmare are interspersed and at times intertwined with sacred subjects. Everywhere Romanesque decoration showed this disconcerting freedom. It seemed to take pleasure in depicting a pandemonium of monsters in holy buildings. This practice led to criticism by St Bernard of Clairvaux.

For we must now consider the famous controversy about art and other matters between Cîteaux and Cluny. St Bernard reacted like a champion of austerity and poverty. If his view was related, in certain respects, to the position previously taken by the iconoclasts and to that later adopted by the Protestants,[5] we must seek to clarify his reasons. He did not fear or denounce worship of false powers but he was concerned rather about the insult given to God by caricaturing His creation and dishonouring His dwelling-place. In any case, he was talking to and for monks. Just as Bernard tolerated wealth for bishops, provided they made a holy use of it, so he showed a certain indulgence with respect to churches intended for lay people. He pardoned in them a certain opulence and frivolity of decoration which he could not tolerate in monastic places. And as a result, we have been given the remarkably pure and bare beauty of Cistercian architecture. This is why such architecture is not further discussed in our book.[6]

[5] Wycliffe repeated for his own purposes St Bernard's denunciations of Pope Eugenius III's pomp: "You are not the successor of Peter but of Constantine".

[6] Up to the early thirteenth century, the Cistercians strictly applied the ban against sculptured works. Then they allowed a crucifix on their altars. (In the twelfth century, they had only crucifixes of painted wood, with no sculptured figure.) In 1253, the general chapter, in the name of "the order's ancient humility and simplicity", had the statues at Royaumont removed, "so that nothing would hint at pride or excess". In the fourteenth century, such bans fell into disuse.

But St Bernard's violent outburst is extremely important for the interpretation of Romanesque iconography. In denouncing the forms he himself saw for their clownish absurdity, he showed that there was no question in his mind of their having an allegorical meaning. It cannot be denied that adornment had developed to a great degree in virtue of a gratuitous law of proliferation. Thus came into play those diversions and genealogies of artistic forms that were studied by Baltrusaïtis or mused over by Focillon. The decorative riches of the most remote regions of the East were copied shamelessly, and, what is more, they took on a new life and multiplied. More frequently than in the past, the "models" found on materials, ivory works, miniatures, even on coins, were turned into stone by sculptors who had become masters of their purposes and materials, and by a form of sculpture which had become a royal art.[7] And their fondness for monsters can be explained less because of a vague feeling of "panic" whose importance has been exaggerated by certain German scientists than because such forms presented outstanding opportunities for decoration.

Yet "symbolistic" art historians began with a correct outlook—one confirmed by the records. When Suger declared that "an unrefined spirit is elevated to the truth only through material forms", he surely included in that catechetical role many more things than we would expect. For the men of the twelfth century, everything was the presence and symbol of God, directly or indirectly. This was the key to the art of that period. It was encyclopedic in nature and found its gift—which was also God's gift—literally everywhere. History was sanctified from beginning to end. Periods of history were only

[7] About the early fourteenth century, ivory works began to copy on a small scale the large iconographic forms which had triumphed on the portals and great retables. The trend that had prevailed for so long had been reversed.

a vast unfolding of Christ. Even profane history was included in that process and illuminated by that light.

What was true for time was also true for space. Everything was God's, even those distant lands on the edge of the earth where unbelievable men and strange animals dwelt, even those remote seas where swam the sirens encountered by bold explorers. Real, exotic animals, such as the monkey, ostrich and whale, were a guarantee, in the animal kingdom, for the existence of the basilisk and leviathan. To display creation in all its wonders was to extol the power of God and remind men that the whole universe's order rested in His hand.

In that perspective and according to such a concept, nothing was inappropriate which might help sum up God's power. Romanesque sculpture was epic as well as encyclopaedic in nature. Now epic poetry is fed on an immense collection of adventures, exploits and voyages, constantly repeated, perfected and embellished. That is indeed what we find on the façades of the churches and under the arcades of the cloisters: all the deeds men have done or are engaged in under God's law and through His favour, all the wonders of the earth and the sky. And let no one begin to reproach sculpture for an imprudent credulousness any more than one might reproach epic poetry for the same reason. Sculpture will reply, in the words of Vincent of Beauvais, that "God has wrought many a wonder on earth that no man can explain. And so we should not refuse to believe anything until we know whether it be false or true".

Moreover, the Middle Ages knew well how to explain everything in their own way. All that was necessary was to discover what a given object was a "figure" of, namely, what it might stand for apart from itself. Ovid or the bestiaries were given a moral interpretation; this meant that a symbolic meaning was discovered for every episode and detail.

That was how allegorical interpretations were often legit-imized.

One of the best-known examples of this was the series of relationships established between the Old and the New Testaments, between Adam and the new Adam, between Eve and Mary, the new Eve—down to the finest details. This theme—the theological bases of which were quite sound but which sometimes received ridiculous applications—gave en-thusiasm and nourishment to people's minds and also to artists until the end of the Middle Ages. For this reason, the moral and spiritual symbolism of animals merits a more de-tailed study.[8]

Such an attitude explains a host of things: The idea of attributing to a detail value as a symbol or recollection, and making this value prevail over any problems which might be presented from the standpoint of verisimilitude or logic. There was no hesitation, during the thirteenth century at Chartres, in representing Pope St Gregory the Great stamp-ing on the feet of a tiny man in a cowl. This man was the pope's secretary and had interrupted the saint while the latter was receiving inspiration from the Holy Spirit (sug-gested by a dove perched on Gregory's shoulder). Similarly, at Amiens, beneath the figure of Zephaniah is a medallion showing a hedgehog going into a house on whose lintel a bird is perched. This scene recalled a verse of the prophet con-cerning Nineveh: "How has she become a desert, a refuge for beasts . . . ! The pelican and the hedgehog will dwell on her capitals." How many cryptograms of this sort there are, and not all of them have been deciphered!

Furthermore, Christ's figure on the tympanums is dis-proportionately large in comparison to the adjacent figures of men, as are the figures of saints in comparison to their executioners, and masters in comparison to their servants.

[8] Cf. Victor-Henry Debidour, *Le Bestiaire sculpté du moyen-age français,* Arthaud, 1960.

Their size is only a symbol of their greater importance. The hand of Christ raised in benediction—and sometimes the hand of the Virgin in majesty holding the Child—might be shown somewhat larger than natural size to indicate the subject's supernatural significance.

Thus a number of apparently ludicrous characteristics of twelfth-century sculpture should be attributed more to the artist's symbolic intention than to clumsiness. For it was not a question of depicting exact reality but of attracting the viewer's attention and making him think. The viewer was forced to think about the Gospel, the last things of man, the parables, the thousand aspects of Creation *through* what was shown him, by interpretation, by a kind of intellectual refraction quite natural in that period. As a result there was a wealth of schematic practices which allowed some surprising liberties. The artist did not flinch from carving a forest on a capital. All he had to do was show a tree, which might be symbolized by a conventional, large flower. A city might be indicated by a few small-sized battlements above a small gate. The River Jordan would consist of three wavy lines, and sometimes the front of a fish would be included so that no one might be in error! The sculptor might even depict breezes, festoons of cushions suggesting clouds, and the very orb of heaven itself.

All the conventions we have just mentioned (many of which were continued into the thirteenth century and even up to the Renaissance) found perhaps their most fully synthesized expression on the portal at Vézelay (1125–1130). In the center of the tympanum, Christ is enthroned in an almond-shaped symbol of glory. In order to show that He is seated, without at the same time causing Him to project above the decorated surface, the artist bent Christ's knees sharply to the left. The garments are adorned with parallel or concentric lines indicating bodily motion through a kind of graphic artifice. Pencils of stone emerge obliquely from His outstretched hands, representing concretely the rays of divine grace which will confer upon the apostles both their mission and the strength to fulfill it. Peter is shown with the keys symbolic of his office, while each of the other apostles carries a book as a sign of Christ's teachings.

Across the full length of the lintel moves a vast procession of human forms. Their legs are spindly, their tunics are stirred by the blast of a great wind. These are all the nations of the earth who are to receive the Gospel. They include peasants, shepherds and archers; pagans leading a bull to sacrifice; pygmies mounting a horse by means of a ladder; and "Panotians" with huge ears. In a kind of archivolt interrupted by the head of Christ are a number of compartments containing other people who are to hear the Good News: the crippled, one-armed and lame; deaf-mutes who have either been miraculously healed or are hoping for a miracle; men with the heads of dogs and Armenians wearing high clogs. The entire composition is framed by a row of round medallions in which the signs of the Zodiac alternate with the type of work appropriate for all the months of the year. We see a siren coiling her fishy tail and an extravagant, circular composition of a dog and an acrobat.

On the pier below, John the Baptist displays the Lamb on a nimbus, while beside him we see the apostles taking leave of one another as they set out on their journey. The standing figure of the Baptist has his legs crossed in the form of an X to show that he is walking. The entire work betrays a strong, dogmatic sense of organization, depicting the radiation of baptismal grace, through water and the spirit, to the most remote and abject representatives of humanity. Equally strong is the sense of plastic composition which radiates from Christ's head, for the whole work's feeling of balance seems anchored on this central element. And yet a sense of tumult runs through all those figures whose wild gestures and feverish poses indicate amazement, impatience

and ecstasy. They represent the stirring of all the sons of
Adam—all of whom have been reborn through the Redemption. Before the wind of divine grace, the whole earth, including "all that had been lost", is now summoned in a loud
voice toward the sublimely silent music radiating from the
divine countenance. At one and the same time we have the
essence of Romanesque order and that of Romanesque disorder.

*　　*　　*

There have been bitter controversies about the chronology
of Romanesque sculpture, and people might well argue about
the proper methods of classification. Thus, during the nineteenth century, Romanesque sculpture was split into various
schools on the basis of geographical regions. And this concept is both correct and convenient. But if we consider
specific cases, we shall see the need for considerable adjust-
ments. For example, where, precisely, is the northern bound-
ary of the Provençal school of sculpture? Should the portal
at Conques be classified as a product of the school of
Auvergne or of Languedoc?

The example of Conques serves as an admirable introduction to another method of classification—one based on pilgrimage routes. Along the roads leading to Compostella,
Rome and St Michael's at Gargano, an obvious relationship
between architecture and sculpture was displayed in monuments erected at great distances. That is because both arts
had not developed in geographical proximity as a result of
influences radiating from central points, but according to a
linear pattern along a pilgrimage route. During the Middle
Ages, when the unity of belief made all continental Europe a
single, sturdy community—Christendom—despite all its tiny
political divisions, men and ideas travelled more readily than
we might be tempted to think.

Finally, it is necessary to point out the influence of religious orders—especially of Cluny, since Cîteaux forbade sculpture. The abbey church at Cluny, the largest in the world after St Peter's in Rome, had a grandiose, carved portal and magnificent capitals. Its ascendancy was noteworthy. Doubtless fewer of the artists here were themselves monks than was at one time believed. In any case, it was a monk named Guinamond who carved and signed his name, in 1077, on the tomb of St Front at Périgueux. Guinamond was from the abbey of Chaise-Dieu, one of the bases of St Robert who had come from Cluny.

It is certain that the earliest Romanesque works must be sought in Languedoc, chiefly at Toulouse. St Sernin and the cloisters of St Stephen's and La Daurade were erected in the closing years of the eleventh century, although not completed until about 1130. At St Sernin we find a marble altar-piece carved by Guilduin, who decorated its border with scroll patterns and also a few figures. In the ambulatory, statues of Christ in glory, the angels and the apostles, also in marble, are characterized by dryness and heaviness of form.[9] The Miègeville Portal retains this same tendency. We can discover, however, all the decorative wealth, all the flexibility of human form, and even the sensitiveness of the human face that are the glories of Languedoc Romanesque on the capitals and statues of the apostles in St Stephen's and La Daurade, and in what remains of the portal at Souillac. All these qualities burst forth in full, monumental power on the portal at Moissac. Also intact at Moissac is the cloister with the great marble bas-relief on its piers; the nine apostles and Abbot Durand; the procession of narrative scenes and purely ornamental compositions on its capitals, surmounting, in alternating fashion, small simple or double columns.

Such decorative compositions were inspired at times by

[9] In Roussillon, as early as the eleventh century, marble sculpture was in a flourishing state. The stone is compact, subtle and, so to speak, without "grain"; this adds an unusual quality to the works.

Arab models from Spain. Once again the East has contributed its sense of form to the sculpture of the West.[10] In any case, there was no border between France and Spain with respect to Romanesque art. The Virgin of Sahagun in the museum at Madrid is a sister to the French statues of the Virgin in majesty. The Romanesque art of Catalonia has a certain unity along both slopes of the mountains, and its brilliant development continued until the end of the twelfth century. The region particularly noted for Romanesque cloisters was southern France and all of northern Spain from East to West. The portals of Compostella—both the Goldsmith's Portal and the Portal of Glory built fifty years later—as well as the portals of Sangüesa and Ripoll, and the one at Avila with rows of statues in its splays: all these monuments offer moving similarities to the masterpieces of France, despite powerful aspects of originality in their over-all design and ornamental details. A rather bitter controversy has arisen as to which works came first, the French or the Spanish. Despite the lively interest it has aroused, the dispute is perhaps pointless.

One fact is clear: Spain is a land blessed with Romanesque sculpture, perhaps because vandalism and restorations, on the whole, have done less damage there than in France. Any canton of Navarre or Catalonia presents, in addition to wonders of the highest order, a host of small village churches whose doors, capitals, and medallions have retained a rustic decoration full of verge and dignity. In France, only the Saintonge region is up to that standard. But do we have anything in France equal to the figures on St Michael's portal at Estella, which dates from the last quarter of the twelfth century? For example, the two angels displaying Christ's empty tomb to the holy women of Jerusalem? Or St Michael weighing men's souls and opposing Satan with all the sweet-

[10] That influence can be detected as far as Auvergne, notably at Puy-de-Dome, whence one of the important "St James's routes" began.

ness and strength of his grace? Or Abraham with a head of curly locks watching like a mother over the souls that recline in his bosom? Do we have anything at all to compare to the six panels in the cloister at Silos? One of them reveals an astonishing boldness of composition: The artist has blocked out a scene of Christ being laid in the tomb. Jesus lies stiffly while two kneeling men arrange his limbs for the sleep of death. Nearby is also a scene of the holy women being greeted by the angel at the tomb on Easter morning. The two moments in time are separated by a line cutting obliquely across the composition. This line is the cover of the tomb which plays a dual role as the stone which will be placed over Christ's dead body and the one the Risen Christ has thrown aside. Thus through an admirable plastic harmony and simplicity of means the artist has symbolically brought together for our meditation all the mysteries enacted between Good Friday evening and the dawn of Easter Sunday.

Spain—especially Catalonia—is also the land of the finest Romanesque sculpture in wood. The Crucified Christ is shown as if standing, His feet joined but not superimposed. He is clothed in a long gown, his eyes are open, his head bears a royal crown rather than one of thorns, and his arms are extended to embrace all Creation and all the creatures of the earth. The earliest Christian art, as we have seen, "skipped" the death of Christ. In this Spanish version we see Christ crucified but beyond death; he lives, loves and reigns.

Later, when representations of the crucified Christ became increasingly "humanized", the artist ended up by showing Him either as an athlete or a molly-coddle. But the faith of the twelfth century chose to show Him in a calm yet triumphant majesty.[11] Also worthy of admiration are the virgins in majesty and altar frontals showing Christ seated

---

[11] Cf. M. Durliat, *Christs Romans,* Tramontane, 1956.

in a *mandorla* surrounded by His twelve apostles. The blind
arcades and little columns of the altar frontals, Mary's throne
and Christ's cross, which is also a throne, are adorned with
guilloches and embellished after the fashion of enamels or
jewels, which, moreover were the direct sources for this
polychrome sculpture.

These large wooden statues, however, can also be sorrow-
ful. On "beams of glory" the suffering, dying Christ[12] hangs
from the gallows. Sometimes his body zigzags in a kind of
lifeless convulsion. Practically naked, he wears only a loin-
cloth. In those works which remain Romanesque in their
solemnity and power of concentration we feel the first
emergence of that fondness for the pathetic which will
achieve such a thrust in Christian Spain. And that is also
true for the figures of our Lady and St John often placed at
the foot of the Cross; by their very stiffness they display a
tendency towards an ardent expressionism.

*   *   *

Just as Toulouse was the main center for the spread of
Romanesque art throughout Languedoc, Cluny had the same
function in Burgundy and at the same time, the first part of
the twelfth century. No vestiges are left of Cluny's great
portal which, like the one at Moissac, contained a vast
apocalyptic composition. But the capitals which formerly
adorned the choir of the abbey church have been preserved.

Those capitals show an unusual originality in subject matter. An "encyclopaedic" aim predominates: Allegorical
figures represent executioners armed with various instruments

[12] The first time Christ was shown *dead* on the cross was doubtless the image in Cologne Cathedral, which is said to date back to
975. The magnificent, wooden, Romanesque sculpture took on
particular brilliance in Spain, but it was to be found all over Europe
in the form of Crucifixions and Depositions. The Depositions usually captured the moment when the nail had just been removed from
one of Christ's arms.

of torture; the eight notes of the scale of sacred music; the four seasons paired with the four cardinal virtues—Spring with Prudence, Summer with Justice, Autumn with Strength, and Winter with Temperance; the four rivers and trees of Paradise—the apple-tree symbolizing the tree of the knowledge of Good and Evil; the grape-vine, or tree of Life; the fig-tree; and the olive-tree. But those themes imply an even more definite aim. We should recall that the abbey was like a spring from which emerged the living waters of the beatific virtues, as well as the notes of liturgical songs prefiguring those of our heavenly abode. For the abbey was a field where harvests of crops and grapes ripened for eternal barns and cellars; it was a garden where flowers of sanctity grew.

The most beautiful of the tympanums—equal to Vézelay's —is the one at Autun, which was preserved because of the scorn it inspired during the eighteenth century. It was walled up, intact, under a thick coat of plaster.

This extraordinary Last Judgement was carved about 1130. It is admirably constructed around an immense central figure. No longer are we confronted by Ezechiel's vision of the four creatures. Instead, we see Christ surrounded by angels sounding trumpets; by St Michael, the weigher of souls; and by St Peter, who leads the elect to the gate of Paradise. On the lintel below, the souls awaiting judgement rise from their graves in expectation of reward or punishment, and they are already in the custody of either angels or demons. Carved inscriptions, including one on which the sculptor has inconspicuously inserted his signature (*Gislebertus hoc fecit*) act as commentaries for this text in which grace and horror confront each other and are blended in a theological and an artistic manner.

A host of more modest works help to reveal the abundance, variety and authority of twelfth-century Burgundian sculpture. For tympanums, one of the favorite themes is the

"Ascension". Christ is borne up by angels whose swallow-like wings fill out the composition with supple motions. On lintels we find either "The Last Supper" or the apostles. And the list of themes for capitals is endless, from scroll patterns and foliage to sacred or secular narrative scenes, including a group of savage beasts and a host of devils whose flame-like mops of hair and wild grimaces border on both farce and terror.

A general characteristic of such works of sculpture is the wide flexibility of its forms which are usually much elongated. Everything promotes a feeling of movement. Garments cling closely to bodies but swirl up in flounces at the hem-line. There is a deliberate emphasis on form as the result of a "graphic" kind of device—tight folds arranged in tiny, parallel or spiral waves.

It is often believed that mediaeval sculpture had a horror of the nude. This is true if we mean the nude male athlete or the sensual female nude of the Renaissance. For the monks, women and the sins of the flesh were the temptation *par excellence,* and such themes could not be handled with too much severity or caution. One of the capitals at Saint-Benoît-sur-Loire depicts Satan offering a woman to St Benedict. How chaste and sober she seems in her long, pleated gown! She might be mistaken for a saint, if it were not for her vile escort.[13] Sometimes, on the other hand, sensual vice is evoked in such a way that it can only strike us with a chill of fear. For example, the "Woman with Serpents" is shown with reptiles and toads crawling over her body and devouring the parts by which she has sinned. Similarly, the animal-like nudity of the devils is something hideous to behold.

In Burgundy, however, Romanesque sculpture presents quite a different feeling for the nude on the lintel of the Last

[13] There are many examples of this chaste way of representing lewdness. Sometimes the temptress can be recognized by a pointed or forked foot protruding from beneath her gown.

Judgement at Autun. Here the dead who are roused by the final trumpet have healthy human bodies. They are not macabre in any way, nor do they look like skeletons. They are not desexed either; at least the women are clearly distinguished by their breasts and long hair from their male companions. But their flesh is, as it were, released from the illusions and servitudes of our earthly life, freed of the enticements and suspicions with which the flesh assails us. The flesh is no longer either tempting or tempted, tyrannical or weak, for it has gone beyond what we call life and what we call death. The Middle Ages carved with the same chisel—in the form of little naked dolls—souls at the moment of dying and bodies at the moment of their resurrection. Souls winging their way towards God and bodies taking on life again are both leaving their temporary *prison*—of flesh or of earth—to rise with the same motion, trembling with joy, towards the glory which will be theirs in common.

Such are the nudes at Autun as they rise from the tomb. (And such were they to be, in the best works of the thirteenth century, although the latter will display somewhat more anecdotal, smiling grace.) When the "way of all flesh" is seen thus, we can quickly understand that all considerations of modesty or immodesty are inapplicable. We might feel that a life-like warmth is lacking in flesh illuminated by eternity. At Autun, however, is a work which in no way merits such a reproach—a reclining Eve.[14] Her body has a gliding, undulating posture, balanced on an elbow and a knee in the rich foliage of the garden of Eden. Her hair flows over her shoulders in long, delicate locks. (Surreptitiously and as if unconsciously, she plucks the fatal apple from a leafy clump in which can be glimpsed the devil's claw and tail.) What freedom and charm in the roundness of her

[14] Eve is almost the only female nude subject portrayed by Christian sculpture. The Eve at Chartres, however, is shown clothed.

curves! How fresh and open is her body! How far removed from any trace of vulgarity or lewdness! [15]

*   *   *

Auvergne has nothing to equal the portals of Moissac, Autun, or Vézelay.[16] The carved tympanum of Notre Dame du Port at Clermont-Ferrand is poor by comparison. The school of Auvergne preferred to decorate lintels and capitals. Its lintels are saddle-shaped, and the place of honour is reserved for Christ or the Virgin. Grouped around the central figure are the apostles at the Last Supper, the Three Magi or other figures.

The capitals, however, are of top quality. They are handsomely located around the ambulatory at Notre Dame du Port, Saint-Nectaire, Issoire and elsewhere. After the carvings of Burgundy, the visitor to Auvergne finds himself in a totally new situation. The subject matter is different to a large extent.[17] The human figure is here more prominently displayed at the expense of plant-like, decorative motifs. Quite different are the materials used and the manner of carving. Auvergne's volcanic stone lacks flexibility and softness.[18] Even the angels are ponderous, and the human

[15] Let us note, also in Burgundy, the figures on St Lazarus' tomb at Autun. Never did the funerary art of that time, which viewed death as the road to resurrection, have a finer subject. These statues were the work of a monk named Martin (about 1170–1189), and they betray a certain debt to the columnar statues of the Île-de-France.

[16] An exception is the extraordinary and delightful tympanum at Conques, which is certainly in Auvergne although just on the border of Languedoc.

[17] Let us mention "The Good Shepherd", a subject often duplicated for reasons of symmetry; the miser seized by devils; the crouching monkey; and the struggle between the Virtues and the Vices.

[18] As Focillon noted, "The materials extended the nature of the soil into the structure of the churches". The same is true also of

figures are heavy. The capital's mass dominates in an absolute manner the distribution of its figures, whose heads project at the corners. In comparison to the Burgundian works, this is a more rustic art-form clinging to its own traditions, some of which appear to go back to the Gallo-Roman period. That does not mean at all that the works of Auvergne are without fantasy or inventive richness. In the confusion of human figures is revealed a lively fondness for the multiplication of forms and, at the same time, for clear, emphatic gestures.

The most remarkable composition, doubtless, is a series of capitals at Saint-Nectaire whose compact scenes elsewhere might have appeared on a tympanum: the Apocalypse and Last Judgement, including angels bearing the "emblems" of our redemption—a cross decorated like a reliquary, the lance and the nails. This astonishing variety of subjects is just what might have been expected in an encyclopaedic anthology of the Gospel, if we may use such an expression. Here are episodes rarely found in the iconography of the period: the Transfiguration, the miracle of the loaves and fishes, Zachary on his sycamore tree, the martyrdom of St Sebastian, and comical scenes such as the one of the "donkey playing a violin". Particularly noteworthy is a piece that is both lovely and curious: It depicts the legend of St Nectarius who, along with Austremonius and Baudimus brought the Gospel to Auvergne. We see the saint—thanks to an angel's help—foiling the snares of the devil disguised as a sailor for the purpose of drowning Nectarius. The saint's boat is perched on a curious pedestal of striated stone representing the Tiber. He is restored to life by St Peter. Elsewhere we see him leaning in a kindly way over a dead man

---

sculpture as shown by the lava and *arkose* of Auvergne, the soft stone of Touraine, and Brittany's granite. A number of capitals in Auvergne are of imported limestone.

whom he himself is bringing back to life. In the background can be seen the very church of Saint-Nectaire, its tiled roof, bays and curved arch. Apart from the devil, all the figures have elaborate curls or locks of hair and deep-set eyes— features which impart an appropriate charm and sense of vigour to this golden legend.

*   *   *

The western region of France, between the Loire and Garonne rivers, has a very different kind of sculpture—one overflowing with decorative profusion, as can be seen even on the modillions and external ornamentation of the windows, especially in the apses. Here the capitals are treated in a style more decorative than narrative, and scant attention is paid to the human figure despite the abundance of animal and plant forms. Lions and birds are depicted in various poses—back to back, in rows, fighting with each other, devouring each other or intertwined. Sometimes they are shown in contorted positions biting or tearing each other or, quite literally, climbing over one another. The viewer's efforts to distinguish the different forms are frustrated by the sculptor's pleasure in first linking and then releasing his monsters in plant-like networks of monstrous proportions. A kind of interchange is established between the animal and plant kingdoms: Bits of foliage seem to clutch each other with claws or lick one another with animal tongues that turn into flowers and buds; and tails, as they grow, turn into vines. A splendid example of this kind of decoration may be found on the capitals of St Eutropius' crypt at Saintes.

Sculpture attains its full glory, however, on the façades. It may be found in the curved grooves of the arches (*voussures*), decorated either, keystone by keystone, in a radiating fashion or, quite differently, by elongated human figures that rise towards the key of the arch like two praying hands joined at the finger-tips. There is no tympanum above the central portal; instead are often found blind arcades flanking the door in a half-circle decorated perhaps with a majestic lion or griffon. Carving overflows onto the façade itself. Often an arcade shelters a large equestrian statue in profile, based on an ancient effigy of the Emperor Constantine. Decorative lions, shown in frisky poses, climb the surfaces of the walls. In outstanding monuments, the whole façade has been arranged in a composite iconographic pattern.

The façade at Angoulême evokes a kind of synthesis of the Church's whole history through the glorious influence of her Founder. At the top Christ ascends into heaven in the presence of Mary and the Apostles, and this scene also represents Christ's triumphant Second Coming. On four small tympanums the apostles are depicted setting out zealously, three by three, to carry the Good News to the world.

At Notre Dame la Grande, in Poitiers, the apostles are arranged in two rows dominated by the figure of Christ in majesty on the gable. Beneath the apostles and dominated by them, in turn, runs a frieze depicting, in consecutive order, the fall of man, a number of the prophets, and scenes of Nazareth or Bethlehem. The archivolts, capitals, and doorjambs are richly carved so that the spectator receives the impression of a kind of huge reredo in stone raised up against the sky. The peculiarly sculptural quality of these figures is hard to judge, because of their elevation and the ravages of time; nevertheless, such carvings make a priceless contribution to architectural monuments. This can be easily judged by examining restorations on which the sculptured decorations have been either eliminated or redone in a bungling way. A work formerly bursting with the power of creativity has become as dry as a draftsman's sketch.

The church at Aulnay in the Saintonge area is a true masterpiece. Its remarkably handsome inside capitals display carvings of Samson and Delilah, Adam and Eve, grif-

fons, elephants and scroll-like decorations. The outside of
the church reveals a true magnificence in the capitals and
archivolts, the window frames of the apse and the elaborate
decoration of the modillions. Its south portal has four concentric archivolts adorned with a host of comic or serious
subjects (among the latter, the elders of the Apocalypse),
while the intrados are enlivened by supporting buttresses in
the form of dwarfs.[19] Finally, the west portal's archivolts
show the signs of the Zodiac, the tasks of the different
months of the year, the wise and foolish virgins together
with their Bridegroom,[20] Virtues trampling on Vices and
angels presenting the Lamb of God for our adoration. On
one side of the portal is a Christ in majesty, and on the
other, the crucifixion of St Peter.

The middle course of the Loire, from Nevers to Angers,
including the regions known as Bourbonnais and Berry,
boasts a goodly number of admirable churches but does not
possess the characteristics of a definite school of sculpture.
Saint-Benôit-sur-Loire is a high spot in monastic history as
well as Christian sculpture. For here it was that the capital
decorated with foliage, which was in the direct tradition of
the Corinthian style, turned into the capital decorated with
narrative scenes. What has been left to us of the sculpture of
Nevers, La Charité and Souvigny shows some influences from
Burgundy or Chartres. And the churches of St Ours at
Loches or St Albinus at Angers show the influence of Poitiers.
The series of capitals at Saint Reverien, Saint Menoux,
Plaimpied,[21] La Celle-Bruère, Gargilesse, Saint-Genou, Isle

---

[19] Above this portal, the broken arch of a window is not adorned
with but rather formed by four warrior figures covered up under
their shield, whose oval is vertically folded in such a way as to
create a jutting angle. These are "groove statues" on the same
principle as the columnar statues.

[20] A closed door separates the Bridegroom from the foolish virgins who are wailing.

[21] Twins of the Plaimpied capitals are found in Nazareth—a direct

Bouchard and Cunault are all of outstanding interest from a plastic and iconographic viewpoint.

Brittany has nothing in the way of Romanesque sculpture worthy of our attention. The Île-de-France, which had contributed the capitals at Saint Germain des Prés, initiated the development of the Gothic style about 1140. Normandy is unimpressive, prefering geometric designs (such as broken staffs, billets, diamonds) to a narrative style of decoration. The only examples worth noting here are the diagonals of the nave at Bayeux, which seem to echo—one wonders how? —Far Eastern art. There are also similarities to Irish interlacing figures—an influence more easily explained.

After the Norman Conquest, the English Channel served as a bridge as well as a barrier, and England became closely tied to its neighbour. The island tradition was blended with new influences and produced quite original works, such as the small columns at Kilpeck or the gilded bronze chandelier at Gloucester (1110), which was wholly constructed of intertwining figures of men, animals and plants. St Michael or St George were favourite subjects on tympanums (for example, at Southwell Cathedral) in the company of a dragon which, even as it became entangled in its own tail, could not help but vividly recall its ancestors' antics on Irish miniatures. A fondness for complex, interlacing patterns and medallions among flowering tendrils is reminiscent of the Saintonge region. The capitals of the crypts in Westminster Abbey and Canterbury resemble Norman works, and certain outstanding carvings are not unworthy of the best French achievements of the period.

The bas-reliefs at Chichester (about 1120) are the work of a master. The figures are highly expressive, their attitudes and faces full of a deep sorrow. The giant figure of Christ

and moving indication of the expansion of French art into far-off lands through the Crusades.

moves forward firmly, beside the gates of Bethany, where he is greeted by the kneeling suppliant forms of Mary and Martha. He has all the animation of the conquerer of death, which he will soon prove by raising Lazarus from the grave and—in a gesture to be repeated in countless bas-reliefs—by delivering from Limbo the saints of the Old Testament. The winged lion on a capital at Winchester has a dignity that recalls the grotesque images formerly at Sainte-Geneviève and now in the Louvre. While not much is left of the carvings at Bury Saint Edmunds, a series of bas-reliefs on a frieze in the cathedral of Lincoln (about 1150) presents Old and New Testament scenes in a carefully planned iconographic style so similar to carvings at Saint-Denis that, according to one theory, the sculptor was a Frenchman. The south porch at Malmesbury is a splendidly extensive piece of decoration, and many of its characteristics may be compared to those of the school of western France: The medallions on the archivolt and the two tympanums recall Angoulême. On the tympanums are shown seated apostles being crowned by an angel whose line of flight passes horizontally above the apostles' heads. Finally, the portal at Rochester is obviously derived from those at Saint-Denis and Chartres, both with respect to its tympanum—on which we see a Christ in majesty with symbols of the four evangelists—and with respect to columnar statues of Solomon and the Queen of Sheba, the prototypes of Christ and His Church.

By contrast, England's carved baptismal-fonts are more numerous and perhaps more interesting than those of France. England's connections to the Continent were not limited to France. The English also visited Compostella and had special links with Flanders and Germany via the Rhine. At Tournai, there was a school of marble workers which enjoyed an exceedingly wide sphere of influence. Monolithic fonts were among their most remarkable achievements, and we find traces of them in England. Their decorations were directly related to the purpose they served. At Castle Frome, for example, we find the Baptism of Christ; at Much Wenlock, Christ walking on the waters; and popular images, such as the Vices and Virtues at Southrop, or elsewhere figures of animals.

Carvings of this sort are the most noteworthy examples of Romanesque sculpture in Scandinavia, at Barlingbo and Sjonhem,[22] in addition to the tympanums, grooves and capitals at Lunds in Sweden. Other examples are also found in Germany.[23]

In German-speaking areas, Romanesque stone sculpture enjoyed a wide but rather indefinite range. From the Rhineland contact was maintained with France, and from Switzerland and Austria, with Lombardy. Romanesque art reached out not only in the direction of Denmark[24] and Sweden but also toward Poland and Hungary. Alsace received the movement directly; often sculpture here achieved originality through a kind of picturesque ugliness of style. Around the apse at Schöngrabern in Austria or the buttresses at Speyer, doll-like figures with big heads, bulbous eyes and shrunken or distorted limbs engage in vague contests with childishly comical beasts. The decorative motifs of men and animals on the façade of St James of the Scotch Church at Regensburg are scarcely an improvement. Somewhat more skill was displayed by a sculptor at Remagen, who had probably visited Lombardy, and the same could be said for the artist responsible for a lofty frieze at Andlau in Alsace. For the portals of Andlau and Sigolsheim, medallions and human

[22] We should also note the hollowed-out wood decorations of Norway, Iceland and Gotland. The door panels and frames at Urnes and Aal with their scroll-patterns and monsters spring directly from the 'Vikings' pagan traditions. Such decorative forms were kept alive until the end of the Middle Ages and even beyond.

[23] At Frankenhorst in Westphalia and at Freudenstadt in the Black Forest.

[24] For example, the portals at Veghy and Oersted, and the tympanum at Ribe showing "Christ Taken Down From the Cross".

figures were cut onto piers and lintels. There was, however, no true feeling of relief; on the tympanum, Christ hands over the keys to St Peter and a book to St Paul. Here the sculptor's aim was rather to fill up space than to make it vibrate with animation. The stuccoes of St Cyriacus' Church in Gernrode and of St Michael's in Hildesheim have a far livelier appeal. Splendid cloisters were built here,[25] and cities like Trier, Speyer and Fritzlar have kept certain works of value. All in all, however, it is not too impressive a display, even including the "cubic" capitals with shallow decorations of which excellent models have survived at Neuwiller-lès-Saverne.[26]

In Switzerland, the eleventh-century capitals at Payerne, which were recently restored to favour, and those at Grandson are not too informative. Fragments preserved at Schauffhausen are more unusual, and the cathedral of Basel possesses four handsome capitals in its choir and two bas-reliefs of top quality.

One of the bas-reliefs depicts six of the apostles under an arcade of three bays; they wear togas in the ancient manner and converse in groups of twos. The other carving is made of red sandstone and is far more agitated in style. It shows the martyrdom of St Vincent in four panels: The saint is whipped and burnt on a griddle; his corpse is first cast aside, then thrown into the sea, and finally gathered up and properly buried. Because of the inventive wealth of details showing, with much grace and verve, the intervention of the angels, devils, executioners and birds, and because of the accuracy of their poses, this work is a true

[25] Examples are found at Paderborn and Bonn in Germany; at Millstadt in Austria; and the remnants of the cloister of Eschau in the museum of Strasbourg.

[26] Romanesque decoration stayed alive for a long time in Germany. A pillar in the crypt at Freising, which dates from the beginning of the thirteenth century, was still covered entirely with a wild design of climbing men and animals.

masterpiece. It is quite apparent that this is Romanesque art, but there has been much controversy over the exact date of its creation. Despite the surprising precociousness of the famous golden altar frontal, which was the glory of Basel Cathedral, it is difficult to place the bas-relief prior to the year 1150.

* * *

Switzerland might lead us directly to Italy, but, first, we shall make a detour through Provence and the Rhône Valley. The architectural decoration here is remarkable—capitals with acanthus leaves, ovoli, fluting, all directly inspired by the art of antiquity. Sculpture with figures can scarcely be seen on the capitals, except in the northern sector at Vienne (Saint-André-le-Bas), at Lyons, and at Vion in the Ardèche region. Carving of this type does appear in cloisters, for example at Saint Trophime in Arles, and on tympanums. One of its special features is the narrative frieze; a splendid example is "The Last Supper" at Beaucaire. This style was developed in a grandiose fashion on the two royal façades at Saint-Gilles and Arles.

At Saint-Gilles, the frieze runs the full length of the church's three portals, making use, as it goes, of three lintels. It presents a rich series of episodes from the life of Christ—scenes full of motion and picturesque elements and solemnity. There is a very lively feeling in the positioning of the figures—their heads were mutilated by the Huguenots —and there is also something Roman in the folds of their togas. The sculptor Brunus and his collaborators managed to give an admirable feeling of authority to the figures placed so solemnly between pilasters. On the lower section of the façade, bas-reliefs of wild animals rending their prey, of Cain and Abel, and of a centaur, archer, and stag—all convey an unforgettable feeling of nervous strength, which is found again in scroll-like ornamentation and decorative animals scattered here and there, such as a Roman eagle, or a bull. The façade of St Trophime at Arles was built at the end of the twelfth century. It is based on that of Saint-Gilles but has a drier, more mechanical style.

The Rhône Valley is a classic meeting point and place for transmitting ideas. The art of Saint-Gilles was not only aware of the sculpture of Languedoc and the sculpture that began to blossom at Chartres in the mid-twelfth century but its own influence also spread much farther than Arles —towards Saint-Barnard de Romans and even as far as Thines in the mountains of the Gévaudan. It showed a connection to the art of Italy in subject matter and manner. To cite just one striking example, sculptors here rediscovered the curious method of using lions as supports of columns. Such motifs may be found all the way from Apulia to Saint-Gilles, by way of Emilia, Lombardy and the French Alps.

*   *   *

In Italy, as we have already seen, the art of sculpture was never completely lost. Byzantine and barbarian influences mingled in the decoration of *ciboria,* pulpits, and grill-works, and the remarkable flowering of the early twelfth century reaffirmed Italy's fondness for sculpture. To a large extent, Italian Romanesque sculpture was more decorative than architectural. Inside churches, it was not associated with a structural element like the capital but rather with sacred furnishings, if we may use such an expression to describe pulpits and tribunes, monumental candelabra, pontifical thrones, baptismal fonts and rood-screens. On the exterior of churches, sculpture first appeared at Pavia and Modena, about 1120 or 1130, in the form of friezes, panels or art motifs fitted into walls. And it was always to retain an effect of veneering. The marble carvings served as a covering and adornment of a building but not as an element of its construction. The Italian tympanums[27] cannot compete with French models. The symbols of the four evangelists may surround the rose window on a gable or may decorate a bishop's throne but they are not displayed in large, triumphal compositions. There is nothing analogous to the "supporting", soaring sculpture of Moissac's piers or to the columnar statue. Italy preferred bare columns supported by a kind of living pedestal—a man, lion, griffon or elephant pinned to the soil by a column.

Another noteworthy aspect was the frequent combination of sculpture with polychrome or gilded inlay. This is a direct legacy from the East. This manner of working marble tends to lead the sculptors away from sculpture towards effects of white lace on black background,[28] or mosaic. Often the sculpture played the role of a mere framework or accent filling out a corner or supporting a shelf, the main focus being the geometrical interplay of the inlayings, as in the pulpits at San Miniato and Sessa Aurunca. On a much larger scale, the upper portions of the Romanesque façades at Lucca reflect the same taste.

On the whole, the expansion of Romanesque art in Italy was not particularly precocious. It lasted, however, well into the thirteenth century. We might cite as the last masterpiece of this style a gilded copper statue of the angel Gabriel now in the cathedral of Parma, which was formerly perched on the peak of the cathedral's bell-tower; it dates from the year 1300. If no Gothic sculpture developed in Italy—at least, none in stone—the reason was that the Romanesque works led directly into the early stages of the Renaissance.

With respect to the geographical divisions of the Romanesque style, there were two particularly favored regions:

---

[27] The lintels, which are amenable to the art of the frieze, are often more interesting than the tympanums.

[28] Cf. the medallion of "Samson and the Lion" in the Civic Museum of Lucca. But this remains sculpture, and what fine sculpture!

(Above) Marble sarcophagus of Junius Bassus in Vatican Grottoes, Rome, A.D. 359, and (below left) detail.

The Archangel Michael, leaf of a sixth-century ivory diptych.

Center door spandrel of the Royal Portal at Chartres Cathedral, France, twelfth century.

Nicola Pisano's marble pulpit at Baptistery in Pisa, 1260.

Adoration of the Magi, detail of pulpit at Baptistery in Pisa.

Base of Crucifix by Claus Sluter, 1405, at Chartreuse de Champmol, Côte d'Or.

Lorenzo Ghiberti's bronze "Gates of Paradise," 1435, at Baptistery in Florence, and (below) detail: *The Story of Jacob and Esau.*

The Creation of Adam, 1430, by Jacopo della Quercia, a panel from main portal of church at S. Petronia, Bologna.

(Left) Donatello's bronze *David,* 1432, and (right) Bernini's marble *David,* 1623.

Tomb of Lorenzo de' Medici showing allegorical figures *Evening* and *Dawn* by Michelangelo, 1534.

Michelangelo's Rondanini Pietà, 1564.

Wooden sculpture *Prayer* by Nina Winkel (1905–   ).

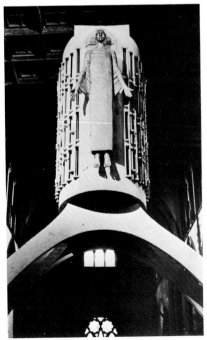

Two Christ figures by Sir Jacob Epstein (1880–1959).

Giacomo Manzú (1908–   ) bust of Pope John XXIII.

all of northern Italy, and Apulia and the Abruzzi in the South. Both these regions were fully open to foreign influences from Byzantium, via Venice, and from Germany and France. The charming capitals of the cloister at Aosta—a final stage on the road to the Alps toward Lyons and Burgundy—are already French. Along the via Emilia are found many works at Borgo San Donnino near Fidenza, at Parma and Modena in the Provençal style. Norman rule in southern Italy and Sicily as well as the role of the Apulian ports in the maritime trade connected with the Crusades left strong traces at Cefalù, Monreale,[29] Bitonto and elsewhere.

The first great Italian sculptor, Guglielmo, was active early in the twelfth century. He adorned the façade of the cathedral of Modena with scenes from the Book of Genesis, depicting human figures full of life and motion. Such figures might be compared to French art of the same period, although they showed distinct traces of Roman influence. His disciple Niccola worked at Piacenza, Ferrara and especially at Verona. The façade of San Zeno at Verona is a priceless treasure.

We have already mentioned San Zeno's superb bronze panels with New Testament scenes completely covering both sections of the door. They date from the eleventh century and came from an earlier church destroyed in the earthquake of 1117. Eighteen plates with Old Testament scenes were added during the twelfth century. Above the door is enthroned a vast tympanum of polychrome stone, sheltered by a jutting portico. On either side is a series of admirable bas-reliefs. To the right is "The Creation of the Animals" from the Book of Genesis—a work of Niccola's hand. A sweet, majestic figure of God stands and blesses a large group of four-footed animals and birds. To the left are scenes from the life of Christ by a Guglielmo who is not to

[29] Aosta and Monreale are the only two Italian cloisters whose capitals have narrative scenes.

be confused with the artist of the same name at Modena. Scenes of the works of the different months and the signs of the Zodiac complete this glorious composition whose monumental effect is not diminished by the wealth of its imaginative details.

In 1178 Benedetto Antelami signed his work on the cathedral of Parma entitled "The Descent from the Cross" —a serious, somewhat dry carving which makes no attempt to be picturesque. Even the soldiers engaged in casting lots for Christ's seamless robe seem full of respect. The sorrow of the Holy Women of Jerusalem and the tender, considerate gestures of Mary, Nicodemus and Joseph of Arimathea are infinitely calm, as is the horizontal flight of two soaring angels. Antelmi may have worked on the rood-screen at Modena, whose "Last Supper" also displays a rather austere nobility.[30]

In any case, Benedetto Antelmi and his studio were responsible for the carvings on the baptistry at Parma. They consist of tympanums and lintels on which figures are placed with a truly classical symmetry, taking advantage of the effects created by empty spaces. Statues of Solomon and the Queen of Sheba are sheltered in rectangular niches, and there is a frieze of circular medallions on which parades a whole horde of beasts full of naturalistic vitality. This group of carvings—to which we should add the lunettes inside the church showing such subjects as "David Playing His Harp", "The Presentation of the Child Jesus in the Temple", and "The Flight into Egypt"—forms a composition of unusual iconographic splendour.

---

[30] The pulpit of this rood-screen, with its symbols of the four evangelists and the doctors of the Church, is more animated. Of a later date, it is the work of Anselm of Campione. In the crypt, a delightful door-jamb depicts the denial of St Peter. The saint is shown warming his hands and feet while a servant girl holding a distaff asks him questions. Inscriptions identify Peter, the servant girl, the fire and the cock.

Carvings inside the baptistry depict the tasks appropriate to the months of the year. We see a series of delightful comic scenes: a man digging in February, riding a horse in May, harvesting in June, threshing wheat in July with the help of two horses, repairing a cask in August, harvesting grapes in September and pruning in December.

Such statuettes in high relief should be compared with the bas-reliefs at Ferrara and Arezzo—works which carry us into the thirteenth century. The same subjects are found later on the sumptuously decorated main portal of St Mark's in Venice. Figurines, animals and the most diverse small creatures fill up the intervals in an animated swirl, evoking our whole daily life: the yearly cycle; the arts and crafts; and the virtues. The correctness of the poses is not obscured by the arabesques and twistings of a most crowded composition. Certainly, this is Christian sculpture. But it is also a splendid tribute to labour, to the coopers, shipbuilders and blacksmiths shown at work with a mallet, auger, gouge or pliers in their hands.

During the thirteenth century, sculptors known as the *Magistri Comacini* carried the Lombard style into the area around Pisa, Lucca and Pistoia. (An example of this development is the pulpit at Barga.) Pisa was later to be the starting point of a revolution which opened the way for an entirely new art style.

In the South of Italy, we should point out—in addition to a number of bronze doors—the handsome reliefs of the life of Christ decorating the shaft of a candelabrum at Gaeta and two altar frontals at St Restituta's in Naples. Worth noting in Sicily are the capitals at Cefalù and Monreale as well as the candlestick in the palace chapel at Palermo; all these are works of the Norman period. Apulia was a cross-roads of many influences: Norman and Burgundian contributions mingled against a background rich in archaic Lombard and Byzantine traditions. Thus archivolts and piers with scrolls, interlacing patterns, monstrous lions and griffons adorn the portals at Trani and Bari, and St Leonard's at Siponto. Direct channels to the East, including Dalmatia and Greece, existed throughout the region, as proved by the portal of Trogir—the work of the sculptor Radovan, who was certainly trained in Apulia.

We have reached the end of our tour through the lands of Romanesque sculpture, and we must now go back to the Île-de-France. Here, about the middle of the twelfth century, the way was being prepared for the appearance of Gothic sculpture.

CHAPTER V

THE GOTHIC PERIOD

The transition from the Romanesque to the Gothic style, if we look for it closely, was imperceptible. That revolution —and it was a revolution—marked no break, and it becomes apparent only if we look down at it from above, as it were, comparing in our minds the over-all characteristics and impressions.

From every point of view, sculpture was freed. Its connections to architecture and theology—even to the stone or wood from which it was made—became more flexible. Its volume was released, its relief surfaces were revealed, and its attitudes became varied and multiplied. The Gothic style opened up its mind to a naturalistic perspective, and—while the Romanesque had played madly with the wealth of its heritage—the Gothic was softly awakened to another style of sculptural life.[1] From Chartres to Rheims and from Strasbourg to Bamberg in the course of a century and a half, sculpture exercised more and more abundantly the impulses of which it felt itself capable. It marvelled at what it was doing (and soon it was to become intoxicated over it).

This development was indicated, quite logically, under all aspects of art. Plants and animals became those of real life, just as the artist could observe them: clover, chicory, chervil and eglantine—with the addition of snails in the

[1] This is what makes it possible to speak of a "Romanesque Baroque style" as well as of a "Gothic archaism".

fifteenth century. The lions and crabs of Amiens are highly accurate in their anatomical details. Even the centaurs no longer had anything extravagant about them, beyond the accumulation of a double realism, partly human and partly horsy. Garments, folds, attitudes, and countenances were relieved of the tricks of stylization and formal conventions. The laws of balance and weight, the impressions of dignity and grace became objects of the most elaborate theoretical interpretations. Henceforth, all objects were rendered more and more from the observation of living forms.

That same realism took hold even of divine subjects— a development possible and legitimate only in Christianity. The Word was a man who had lived, suffered and been put to death. Mary was only a woman in real life. Thus the artists had a solid theological basis for representing Christ and Mary in the most humanly true and moving manner. Even God the Father became an old man, cruelly observed even to His wrinkles, drooping eye-lids and jowls in certain wooden statues of the late Gothic period in Germany. Later, Protestant criticism would have a splendid time criticizing representations of God and the saints which created impressions that were a curious mixture of too much naïveté on the one hand and too much refinement and technical proficiency on the other. As a result, their religious effect was either suspect or completely debased.

The views reported so briefly here encompass the destiny of Christian sculpture throughout the Gothic period in the widest sense of the term—that is, up to the early sixteenth century. But it is important to distinguish its developmental aspects over more than three and a half centuries, according to the different generations and countries (with the exception of Italy). They present an inexhaustible gamut of diversity, contrasts and contradictions. Who would admit, at first glance, that the same term "Gothic" could be applied to the carvings on the rood-screen at Chartres and the reredo at Fromentières? To the Virgin at Saint-Denis and the one carved by Claus Sluter? To the Christ on the Cross at Sens and the one at Perpignan? And, for over-all impressions, to the façade at Bourges and St Vulfran's at Abbeville?

Continuity is perceptible, nevertheless. A chronological study of certain major subjects, such as Christ on the Cross, the Virgin, or the tombs, shows this clearly. It does not extend as far as the curious temporary symbiosis between the Gothic and Renaissance styles, which was not so marked for sculptors as for architects.

If time modified everything, geography also had a role to play. National temperaments showed through or, as the case might be, reabsorbed the details of the style. French in its origin, Gothic art spread through the lands of northern Europe in a princely manner in one place, and in a bourgeois fashion in another. It remained an imported style in all of southern France and even in Spain. Painted wooden statues developed in Spain according to a local style which the influence of Italy—a land which the Gothic style scarcely penetrated—was later to revitalize and then to be launched again in its own fashion. But all this does not contradict at all the evidence of a certain unity. Commercial and artistic interchanges were intensive, favored by political and religious events as diverse as the Crusades, the war against the Albigensians, the Hundred Years War, the removal of the papacy to Avignon, and the territorial expansion of the Dukes of Burgundy.

The first masterpieces that opened the way for the new style appeared in the Île-de-France between 1140 and 1155. The façade of St Denis, whose design was completed by Suger, has been so mistreated by vandals and restorers that it is mentioned only for historical reasons. But the royal portal of Chartres is intact. This grandiose work is the turning-point and doubtless the summit of all Christian sculpture in the Middle Ages.[2]

The royal portal at Chartres is directly connected to the monumental art of the great abbeys of Burgundy and southern France. On the central tympanum, the Christ of the Apocalypse, surrounded by symbols of the four Evangelists, is enthroned above the apostles. On the tympanum over the right-hand door, the Virgin is seated in majesty between two angels carrying censers; she holds the Child, who offers a blessing. On the left-hand tympanum, Christ rises from a cloud between two astonished angels, while other angels, suspended between heaven and earth, point Him out to the seated apostles, who raise their heads, just like the apostles of Moissac. The signs of the Zodiac and the tasks of the months of the year are shown in rows in the adjacent grooves. All these carvings are completely Romanesque.

Along the full length of the façade, a continuous frieze—interrupted only by the three doors—unites the movement of the splayed doorways. It relates the whole life of Christ in small animated scenes arranged under a festoon of tiny arcades that are worked in depth. The frieze is formed, in fact, by a series of contiguous capitals crowning the columns which rhythmically mark the lower portion of the façade. These columns are the famous columnar statues—an ingenious innovation. Contained within the same stone block as the shaft which they animate, and resting their feet on a slight, oblique base, these figures are not caryatids at all. Their heads are free and upright, their bodies rise effortlessly. The statues were not fixed where they are in order to break the overly abstract design of upright lines. As we try to describe them we are struck by the poverty of all verbal expression. They are nothing if not forms of quiet harmony, yet to characterize them we are forced to stum-

[2] Cf. Henry Daniel-Rops, *Le Porche du Dieu fait homme,* Paris, 1953.

ble over contradictory phrases. There is a perfect rigidity
about these figures that are more fluted than clothed; there
is a perfect flexibility in their motionless motion; there is
a strict monotony and yet a delicate variety to their com-
pressed attitudes. Their faces exhibit a kind of empty indifference and, at the same time, a fulness of contemplation;
their smiles do not really smile at all; their sealed lips sing
of silence and proclaim a secret that remains a secret—a
mystery in broad daylight. And if we realize that these are
heralds of the Old Testament, standing at attention before
Christ's triple human and divine revelation on the tympanums, then all these figures acquire an admirable, spiritual
logic. They are at one and the same time glorious and humble, royal personages and people of humbler rank, indis-
pensable yet interchangeable figures.

The purely decorative carvings have found refuge on the
lower portions of the columns and at the tops of inter-
mediary small columns adorned by plant and geometric
designs of infinite variety. The grooves or piers shelter
figurines that complete this group of images in an absolutely
novel way. They include, for example, the liberal arts—
studious female forms accompanied by the pagan Sages who
paid them honour.

At Chartres, both in the organization of the forms and
the concepts, there appears a power of unity, totality and
logic—from the most essential and imposing aspects down
to those that are most tiny and casual. This wonder is all
the more surprising since the façade we have before us is the
result of different compromises and renewals, the work of a
number of studios. But we have not reached the era of the
great cathedrals, where successive master-builders learned
how to collaborate with each other—at times over a period
of two generations—without abdicating their personalities.
They were swept along by all the living powers of Christendom—the royal house, bishops, clerics, guilds and town or-

ganizations which, with joyful hearts, offered funds, meditation, work and prayers for their common masterpiece.

Chartres had transformed the Romanesque heritage, and the new style spread rapidly. Almost everywhere in France, even in places where the Romanesque tradition was firmly maintained, the second half of the twelfth century bore witness, in many details even if not in the over-all design, to the prestige of Chartres. The major works we can admire are a statue of the patron of the priory at Saint-Loup-de-Naud in the Brie area; a mysterious head of a king with closed eyes in the Beauvais museum; a statue in the Meaux museum from the tomb of St Faron, whose quiet authority recalls the most beautiful Greek works of the sixth century before Christ. We must add the charming scenes from the upper lintel of St Anne's Portal at Notre Dame of Paris and the carvings at La Charité-sur-Loire.[3]

The next stage of development was also in the Île-de-France—at Senlis, in 1190. From this time until the end of the thirteenth century, the statuary of the great French cathedrals was elaborated. Included are Laon, Sens, Chartres (where the north and south portals were carved between 1200 and 1250), Paris, Amiens, Rheims, Cambrai (now destroyed), and Bourges (whose west façade dates from about 1280). At the same time, Poitiers, Bordeaux, Bazas, Dax, Auxerre, Sées and many other episcopal cities embraced the new art style. Among them were Saint-Yves de Braisne at Longpont, Larchant, Rampillon, Villeneuve-l'Archévêque, Germigny-l'Exempt, Semur-en-Auxois, Saint-Thibault and a host of churches, not to mention those destroyed or mutilated beyond restoration.

It is better, at this point, not to attempt a detailed study

[3] Let us point out the rather little-known Virgin in the museum of Saint-Maur-les-Fossés, who is shown offering her breast to the Child. This is one of the first examples of this theme.

of the subject, for it would be almost useless. Certain points merit particular emphasis, however.

It is possible to speak of a "classical period" of sculpture in the thirteenth century, during the reign of St Louis (1226–1270). Such a concept is attractive, especially since it seems to indicate a developmental curve somewhat analogous to that of Greek sculpture. There is, indeed, a kind of "comparison" between the *xoana* of the seventh and sixth centuries before Christ and the Romanesque "enthronements" or columnar statues, between the contorted expressionism of the "Laocoön" or Pergamene sculpture and the wild excesses of fifteenth-century German Gothic works. The artist seeks to achieve his effect either by refraining from emphatic gestures or by giving full freedom to them. Between the two tendencies, there is room for a "classical" art —the art of Phidias or Praxiteles, that of Amiens or Rheims,[4] which knows at one and the same time how to free and yet retain the physical expression of a pose, and the moral expression of a feeling. It is an art that finds its own style by going beyond all stylizations of rigidity or exuberance. It is classical because it soars majestically above all classifications.

Such a view is doubtless too satisfying for the human mind, and studies by specialists have pointed out its weak points. But the role of specialists is always to emphasize the complexity of factors and thus to keep us from reaching any conclusions. All the same, if there is any meaning to the term "classical period of Christian sculpture"—and why shouldn't it have a meaning?—then we ought to apply it to the thirteenth century. Sainte-Beuve used the word "classical" to describe "literatures in a state of health and happy

---

[4] It was long ago observed that the folds of the garments of the "Visitation" at Rheims are reminiscent of the finest examples of clothed statuary in ancient times.

flowering, fully in accord and harmony with their period of history, their social patterns, and the principles and dominant powers of their society; satisfied with themselves—and let us clearly understand that by this we mean satisfied with their nation, their time and the society in which they are born and flourish—literatures which are, and feel themselves to be, at home, in their own groove, not rejected, not disturbing, not having anxiety as their guiding principle." Does not this passage seem to describe the sculpture of the thirteenth century?

That sculpture belongs to Christendom and refers everything to God: nature, the works and the days, the secular sciences, the past and the future, the earth, sky, plants, animals and men. All these things are God's creatures, which are offered to the Creator; they are submissive to His precepts or readopted by His grace.

That sculpture is oriented toward the community in its elaboration and aims. We do not have the name of a single one of those talented sculptors. Their position in life did not distinguish them from their comrades the stone-cutters, and if, as is probable, a certain great master-builder whose name we have was himself the carver of important pieces of sculpture, we do not have explicit knowledge of this fact. Works of co-operation and competition, the cathedrals were a remarkable crossroads of pride and humility, of local pride and a worker's pride in what "we" do as opposed to what "I" do—for the glory and service of God.

That sculpture is loyal towards the established authorities. It is not at all anticlerical, nor is it socially critical or clandestinely "democratic". Such an attitude would be materially and spiritually impossible. Neither is it at all obsequious. How could it be, since it sees everything—even kings and bishops—in the light of Christ, the King of kings and Priest of priests? And if the great of this world are shown on their way to hell, wearing their crowns and mitres, the purpose was obviously not to glorify them or to promote a revolution. Rather it was to recall to everyone and to the great of this world that, while all Christians have their share in the promises of the Gospel, all of them—and the great more than others—are pursued by the Gospel's threats. Thus that sculpture maintains an admirable equilibrium, for it has a sense of *respect* for the grandeurs of the established order as well as for the natural and supernatural grandeurs. But *respectability* is unknown to that sculpture, which is what makes it so lusty, bold, fresh as well as so noble and restrained.

It is also a happy art. Not at all because it brings sweetness, but because it bears witness to a religion of hope. Evil, suffering and death have neither the first nor the last word. Evil is temporary, and its triumphs are beaten in advance; or, if it is beyond remedy for those who will have chosen their own damnation, it is limited. Satan enchains men but is himself a chained power, checkmated on all sides by Christ in Limbo, by St Michael, the weigher and saviour of souls, by the prayers of Mary and even of the worst sinner. If Christ suffers and dies on the Cross, His suffering brings peace and His death brings life. The figures of the dead at Bourges and Rampillon rise joyfully on their way to heaven, and those whom hell awaits pass almost inconspicuously. The tomb is only the quiet resting place on the threshold of joy. The carved figures of the dead are statues of living persons: Bishops are shown blessing, kings holding sceptres in their hands, queens their books of hours. When a funeral ceremony is depicted, the procession is a serene one. If the bite of time, which devours all flesh, is evoked, as on a tomb at Joigny, we see the story of Barlaam interpreted in so calm a pastoral light that its subject matter is not readily identified.[5]

[5] The principal tombs of thirteenth-century France (apart from those at St Denis) are at Fontevrault, Carcassonne, Jouarre, and

Finally, that sculpture is on a human scale—precisely because it is "divine". Christianity teaches that man is made in the image of God, and that God became man. God and man are, in some way, of the same family. There is an eternal scope to man, just as there is a temporal existence in God. Thirteenth-century statues interpreted both these facts. Holiness radiated in the grace of the countenances, and that supernatural halo did not deprive the faces of any masculine vigour or feminine sweetness; it was only its consecration. A true warrior was depicted by the St Theodore at Chartres or by the knight receiving Communion from Melchisedech at Rheims; true young ladies, by St Modesta at Chartres and St Olpha at Amiens; a true young ecclesiastic, by St Stephen at Sens; a true young mother, by the "Gilded Virgin". The Child Jesus or Christ offering His blessing and teaching mankind is, indeed, the One who, as Charles Péguy reminded us, was not just someone in a "mythology", for "He walked along the highway like an ordinary man; His feet trod the earth." And the angel Gabriel, God's messenger, is a youth of stone or wood [6] whose wings do not keep him from standing on our earth.

The great sculpture of the thirteenth century renounced conventional and showy methods of proclaiming majesty, power and sanctity (including the formalized device of enlarging the figures).[7] It had acquired sufficient strength and

Aubazine. Amiens is famous for bronze tombs. England has preserved a large number of tombs in Purbeck marble at Exeter, Worcester, Ely, York and elsewhere. In Spain, there are examples in the cathedrals of León and Burgos and the church at Villalcázar de Siga. In the fourteenth century, statues of the dead are shown with closed eyes. The loveliest tombs are in Spain and Portugal (for example, the tombs of Don Pedro and Inès de Castro at Alcobaca).

[6] As in the church at Humbert in the Pas-de-Calais region.

[7] The architects at Beauvais, to be sure, were tempted by a fondness for gigantic forms. The Christ of the Apocalypse on the Romanesque tympanums had been a colossal figure, and images of

depth of knowledge "concerning the meaning of the inner man" to associate with ease—one might say with marvelous ease—God on the same level with ourselves and ourselves with God.

* * *

The royal portal of Chartres had an immense influence. Columnar statues are found on the portal of Sangüesa in Navarre, and later at Rochester in England, at Tournai, and even as far away as Pecs in Hungary. The Christ in glory of Chartres has its echo at Rochester, and Chartres' Virgin in majesty was mirrored at Vezzolano in Lombardy. The prestige of the French studios, especially the one at Rheims, was equally great. The tympanum of St John's at Bruges and the carvings at Lausanne are proof of this. The movement spread to Bohemia and Hungary, where the apostles on the gable at Jaak are of French workmanship. In Scandinavia, we may mention the statue of St Olaf at Tanum and the carvings on the west façade of the cathedral of Trondheim. At Cosenza, in Italy, the tomb of Isabel of Aragon, who died while returning from the Eighth Crusade in 1270, is the work of French artists.

In Spain, the marriage of the Infanta, Blanche of Castille, to Louis VIII, revived traditional links to France. Monumental portals of the cathedrals of Burgos and León and the collegial church at Toro display an over-all composition, beauty and charm of detail that remind us of French master sculptors. The grooves of Tudela's "Last Judgement"—the only portion to survive—the Precious Door of the cathedral of Pampeluna, the portals of the church of the Holy Sepulchre at Estella, the church at Ujue, St Mary of the Kings at

St Christopher were so, too, during the fifteenth century. But this was never the case for thirteenth-century statues; even plant-like decorations respected the size of the foliage on which they were modelled.

La Guardia and the cathedral of Ávila, all continued the development in Spain of a sculptural style imported from France. In the adornment of the cathedral of Toledo, this style mingled with influences derived from the new Pisan style.

In England, the tradition of the royal portal was not adopted, as had been the case in France, Spain and Germany. Decorative carvings were widely distributed on the façade or nestled in every corner. Such art soon took on a dainty quality that was to increase with the passage of time, as can be seen from the celebrated series of the thirty angels in Lincoln Cathedral's choir. But the sculpture at Wells and Lincoln is admirable in its major subjects and often charming in its minor ones, including Wells' large statues and charming quatrefoils with their accompanying narrative scenes and such works at Lincoln as "The Church", "The Synagogue" (both now unfortunately mutilated) and the wise and foolish virgins arranged in small loges within the foliage of the grooves.

As the French sculptural influence expanded into Germany, especially into Westphalia, Saxony and Thuringia, it met definite local tendencies. Even in cases of direct imitations of French models, a striking degree of originality was retained. Forms were emphasized, characteristics were stressed, lusty mimicries and realistic details—even absurd ones—were cherished. The discreet grace and mysterious reticence of Amiens or Rheims are scarcely found in the rich compositions at Paderborn, Münster, Magdeburg, Freiburg, Bamberg, Naumburg and Freiburg-im-Breisgau. Although the famous statues of "The Church" and "The Synagogue" at Strasbourg are from the school of Rheims, the Germanic character of this sculpture is strongly marked at times, for example, on the tympanum of "The Death of the Virgin".

We should need more space than is available here to classify in detail the German achievement, especially at Bamberg, where the works of different hands and periods are gathered. The high-relief carvings of the choir enclosure which date from about 1230 are animated and loquacious —qualities that are to be found in the art of the fifteenth century.

Twenty years after the carvings on the "Portal of Adam", other works of sculpture appeared inside the church—"The Church", "The Synagogue" and an equestrian figure believed to be St George—have a serene purity and an admirable sense of balance.[8]

At Naumburg, twelve remarkable statues dating from about 1260 adorn the choir. They are unique for the period, since they depict benefactors of the cathedral, true laymen lacking the sacred quality they might have gained through being saints or having imperial rank, as was the case for the statues at Bamberg of Henry II and Cunegunda.[9]

The development of Gothic sculpture after the thirteenth century was rather simple, despite the enormous proliferation of individual works. Before evoking briefly the main centers of production, we shall consider this development under four headings.

These headings are directly related to the movement of men's minds and institutions as shown by the following factors: the increase of secular power; religious confusion due to the debasement and splintering of papal authority; a

[8] Large equestrian figures had already been carved in France, for example, the statue of King Philip Augustus at Notre Dame of Paris. But no figures in France can be compared to Bamberg's nude Adam and Eve or the statues of the apostles raised on the shoulders of prophets in the splayed doorways.

[9] The struggle between the papacy and the Holy Roman Empire had its echoes in art. At Aix-la-Chapelle, the reliquary of Charlemagne ordered after Emperor Frederick I ("Barbarossa"), on his own authority, had canonized his illustrious predecessor, is adorned with statues of fourteen emperors—not apostles or prophets. The important point was to affirm the sacred character of lay power.

sense of insecurity caused by the Hundred Years War and the great epidemics; the substitution by the mendicant orders of a popular Christian propaganda along emotional rather than intellectual lines for imposing theological syntheses; and the phenomenal enrichment, towards the end of the period, of princes, cities and businessmen—a development which led to a syphoning off of the profits of an early economic revolution. All these important factors particularly affected religious sculpture, since sculpture was decidedly more popular than painting at the time and thus even more sensitive to social conditions than painting.

Our first heading, or consideration, is of a technical nature. Sculpture tended to lose its monumental quality. Beginning in the early fourteenth century, entire sections of the façades of Rouen and Lyons cathedrals were covered with medallions that depicted, casually and side by side, sacred or profane subjects; even comical themes were seen. Keystones, jambs, bases and consoles were laden with carvings. The capital—an admirable meeting-place for the arts of sculpture and architecture—offered space for trivial designs in the form of leaves. Such works were merely a sculptor's pastime, and they detracted from the architectural line.

Great statuary, for its part, became separated from its background. Statues attached to piers disappeared, and the works became isolated. Beginning in the thirteenth century, in the Sainte Chapelle at Paris and later at Carcassonne, figures are observed inside the building and halfway up the piers whose upward sweep they interrupt. The lovely statues of the apostles from Rieux (1330–1350) seem scarcely out of place today in the Augustinian Museum at Toulouse, for they already belong to an art-form which will soon convert the church into a museum. That does not mean that the feeling for over-all impressions disappeared; works of sculpture were conceived rather as carved tableaux on certain

tympanums[10] and on the panels of choir enclosures. Elsewhere, such works sought to achieve a monumental quality
of their own, tucked away in the corner of a church as
was the case for tombs and carved groups depicting "The
Entombment of Christ". The large reredo of carved, gilded
wood [11] laden with figures and scenes synthesized the fondness for carved tableaux and the concern for "movable monumentality".

Our second consideration is the growth of secularization.
In the thirteenth century, statues of laymen, even royal
figures, were rare, but they became increasingly numerous.
Private sanctuaries built by powerful persons in their dwell-
ings, or chapels donated by them in churches contained
many images of their patrons. Such sculpture, like the kind
we find on tombs, may be technically Christian, but personal
or family pride plays a larger role in it than religious fervour.
The famous portrait of Charles V, formerly in the church of
the Celestines and now in the Louvre, has nothing Christian
about it apart from the monarch's affection for the religious
establishment he had endowed and the miniature church in
his hand, which symbolizes his role as its protector.[12]

The fondness for portraiture was so keen that it invaded
even religious subjects. The Virgin and saints often borrowed
the features of models offered to the artist or imposed upon
him. In addition, the predilection for directly observed de-

[10] Thann, the cathedral of Bern (by Erhard Kung, 1490), Neu-
ville-lès-Corbie (1530).

[11] The reredo was originally of painted stone, for example, the
one from Carrières-sur-Seine now in the Louvre; it dates from the
twelfth century. Examples of a later date may be found which are
a curious translation into stone of wooden polyptyches. Such a one
is the reredo of St Bartholomew in La Seo at Urgel.

[12] In contrast is a twelfth-century group now in the Louvre that
depicts Jacques de Vaudémont embracing his wife; he has just re-
turned from a crusade after sixteen years, during which time she
has refused to believe him dead. This is an admirable Christian work
—one of the most moving pieces dedicated to the virtues of hope,
fidelity and chastity, both conjugal and sacramental.

tails transformed into "life-like scenes" many episodes from the Gospels and the Golden Legend, but at the risk of submerging their spiritual message.

This brings us to our third consideration: the startling growth of emotional realism tending towards tenderness or suffering. Sculpture became sentimental and appealed to a new kind of involvement on the part of the spectator. The Virgin became more flexible; while still chaste, her shape was outlined with a boldness that sought, for the first time, to make her "charming"—and it achieved its aim. She plays with her nursling Son, caresses Him or pinches His cheek. He amuses Himself with an apple or bird, and there is nothing about these objects to remind us of the globe or the Holy Spirit in the form of a dove. He may seek to undo His Mother's bodice or leap about as if trying to escape her grasp. The warmth of a family scene, an artisan's intimate circle or the joys of family life—with the accent more on health than holiness—are the aims of many carved groups representing either the three Marys with their many children or a carpenter's workshop in which the Child Jesus pretends to work among the wood shavings.

Let the artist but place two pieces of wood together in the form of a cross and at once a completely new perspective is opened for our feelings—the Passion, to which the spectator is bound by a kind of fascination. Here is the "Man of Sorrows", crushed beneath the blows of whips and a crown of thorns, stumbling under the burden of a heavy beam. We see Him stupefied beneath His cloak of scorn or seated on a stone, nude, bleeding, with bound hands, as the executioners open up the soil (at the same time revealing Adam's skull) in order to erect His cross. We see Him shrunken, dejected, prostrated by an ignominious death. Here is the Virgin of Sorrows holding on her knees the dead body of her Son, rigid in tearless grief or weeping inexhaustible tears. Here is what the Germans call the "Throne of Grace"—a kind of portrait of the "Sorrow of God the Father"; God is a majestic and distraught old man, offering to men His crucified Son or holding His supine form in His lap. Here is "The Sorrowful Christ", upright in the tomb, nude, with wounded hands and side; He is shown in a kind of phantom existence, stripped of all glory and power, between death and resurrection.

Death haunted the end of the Middle Ages. Although the Dance of Death was never a theme of sculpture, figures shown as cadavers began to appear on tombs in the late fourteenth century (for example, the statue of Cardinal La-brange dating from 1402 in the Avignon museum). Limp bodies were depicted, their flesh eaten by corruption and worms, nude or half-clothed in winding sheets from which protrude hideous shapes or fleshless bones. In place of the quiet, almost happy funeral scenes of the thirteenth century, the mourners of Burgundian sculpture display beneath their hoods all the attitudes of distracted grief. Even the angels weep beside the dying or dead Christ, as if the darkness that covered the heavens at the third hour on Good Friday was to be without a dawn. In all these aspects, the sculpture of the late Middle Ages left behind supernatural grandeur, silence, joy and beauty in order to devote itself to prettiness or horror, compassion or terror.

Finally, the form of piety changed, and art marked that development, following and guiding it at one and the same time. The works of mystics and contemplatives, the spread of devotion to the Christmas crib, the Rosary, and the Passion, including the adoration of the Cross: All these trends proceeded at the same rate, and required—if we may use such an expression—a new iconographic repertory. The devotion to the Virgin underwent a remarkable evolution with respect to all aspects of her earthly and eternal destiny, from the Immaculate Conception to her Coronation in heaven, including authentic or apochryphal incidents in her life as a child, young girl and mother. Hence the countless examples of the Virgin's "Annunciation", "Motherhood",[13] "Assumption" and "Coronation". The mysteries that properly belonged to Christ were also associated with her, through the Rosary as well as all sacred history through the tree of Jesse. Let us note also the "Virgins of Mercy", depicted as sheltering all humanity beneath their mantle. Another theme was the "Marian Trinity"—St Anne, Mary and Jesus. All these subjects are moving, charming and theologically correct, but they contain all too many elements that later were to nourish complaints by the Huguenots about "Mariolatry". No title in the litanies of the Virgin was without its interpretation in wood or stone. Devotion to the Five Wounds was not always limited to the crucified Christ or the God of Mercy; the wounds themselves might be carved on an escutcheon as if on Christ's coat of arms. The same treatment was given to the Holy Countenance as it appeared in relief on Veronica's veil.[14]

Devotion to the saints became diversified and specialised. First came those who gave protection against a tragic death: SS Christopher,[15] Barbara, Roch, Antony and Sebastian were invoked against epidemics. Very popular were the Healers, who were associated—especially in Germany—in a kind of college known as the Fourteen Helpers. If we add the saints (both male and female) chosen sometimes for bizarre reasons as patrons of different kinds of brotherhoods, crafts, vocations and interests, we can understand the proliferation of statues. Such images were equipped with

[13] Here and there are to be seen even portrayals of the "Virgin of Pregnancy". Later on, they were put aside as unseemly.

[14] See the church at Écouis. Such subjects are rather frequent on the calvaries of Brittany.

[15] It was said that a prayer made before one of St. Christopher's images would protect a believer from the danger of dying that day. Hence, the images were of huge size and placed outdoors for greater convenience. A famous one was at Notre Dame of Paris.

the attributes peculiar to each saint and recalling his speciality[16] or even showing him in action: for example, Crispin
and Crispinian in a shoemaker's shop and Hubert hunting
a stag. All are dressed as if they were the artist's contemporaries.

*   *   *

Everything we have noted above received its most complete and violent—but not always most beautiful—development in German sculpture, especially the wood carvings.
The crucified Christ, raised high on His beam of glory at
the choir entrance between the Virgin and St John and
sometimes accompanied by Mary Magdalene, the two thieves
and Longinus, was an art-form inherited from the twelfth
century and which had spread throughout Europe.[17] But
the crucified Christs carved in the Rhineland in the early
fourteenth century have a fierce and powerful beauty. Nailed
to a roughly hewn, forked tree, these figures hang with full
body-weight, head deeply bowed, arms forming a U, hands
shrivelled, knees bent, stomach caved in and rib-cage bursting—they are an almost unbearable image of suffering even
in death.[18] By comparison, the countless Swabian statues of
saints or episodes from the Passion, especially the swooning
Virgin or Virgin of Mercy, and St John resting his head on
Christ's shoulder, seem pale despite their moving expressionism.[19]

[16] For example, St James as a pilgrim; St Margaret, the patroness
of women in childbirth, shown being expelled from the belly of a
dragon; Cosmas and Damian as physicians.

[17] For example, to Poland, where there is a very complete composition at Biecz; to Norway; and to England.

[18] For example, St Mary's of the Capitol, Cologne; St Severinus';
the Schnütgen museum. Two such carvings reached France through
unknown channels: the Christ of Brioude, and the "Devout Christ"
of Perpignan.

[19] Let us point out, however, the wooden statues of Christ riding
a donkey, made for use in the Palm Sunday processions and known

A number of great sculptors should be mentioned by name:[20] Gerhard of Leiden (1420–1474), a vigorous portraitist who worked at Strasbourg, Trier and Vienna; Jörg Syrling of Ulm; Michael Pacher; Veit Stosz (1447–1533), a wood-carver who was as much a Pole as a German—he worked for twelve years on the extraordinary main altar at Cracow and then presented Nuremberg with an "Angelic Salutation" (1517), which hangs in an arresting fashion above the nave, surrounded by the fifty beads of the Rosary, the Joys of the Virgin, and crowned by God the Father offering His blessing; Adam Krafft (1450–1509), who carved in stone an enormous, open-work tabernacle at St Lorenz' in Nuremberg and the heavier panels of the Way of the Cross for St John's Cemetery; Tilmann Riemenschneider (1468–1531), who carved in sandstone a statue of Eve—nude, looking a little chilly and affected but daintily graceful—in the cathedral of Würzburg, as well as the stone tomb of Emperor Henry III; and Peter Vischer (1460–1529), a bronze-caster, influenced by the Italian Renaissance, whose tomb of St Sebald is at Nuremberg.

We must also include such names as Bernt Notke, whose statue of Christ and an Adam and Eve group are at Lübeck and whose St George is at Stockholm; Heinrich Duwermann, whose reredo of the Seven Sorrows is at Kalkar; and the master of Brisach known as "H.L.". All three artists rebelled against the influence of ancient or Italian models; they raised their exuberant forms to a wild kind of Baroque style which retained, however, a mediaeval, Nordic feeling. While Italian and Spanish sculptors showed God and the saints soaring among volutes of draperies and clouds, the Germans

---

as *Palmesel*. They possess a sweet kind of serenity, which is rare for German works. An example can be seen in the museum at Colmar.

[20] Cf. L. Réau, *Peter Vischer et la Sculpture franconienne du XIVe au XVe siècle,* Plon, 1909.

placed them in a confused tangle of spirals, thorns and spikes.

England contributed choir-stalls and many tomb statues with unusual details, such as a fondness for depicting the figures with their legs crossed. This rich statuary was generally placed along church walls, for example, in a composition of ninety-six figures in Henry VII's chapel of Westminster Abbey—a complete, iconographic collection of mediaeval saints (1502–1512). The prophets wear extraordinary head-coverings; St Matthew has eye-glasses; and St Sebastian and the archers are shown twice. But England's most noteworthy works are the Nottingham alabasters of the fourteenth and fifteenth centuries. They consist of statuettes or small, rectangular panels intended as adornments on the sides of tombs, or as reredos when enclosed by wooden frames. Such light-weight carvings were easy to transport and enjoyed a lively success all over Europe. Numerous examples are found in France, especially in Brittany, and at various places from Portugal to Hungary, Italy and Iceland.[21] The forms are gracious but slender, the poses studied and rather affected, the faces vaguely sombre or smiling. This pious sculpture, originally painted and gilded, was turned out on a mass basis, and the charming or amusing details in which it abounds lost much through monotonous repetition. Such carvings are related to ivory work, although on a larger scale, and are more facile in workmanship.[22]

Returning to France, we shall restrict ourselves to the key works and principal artists. Right away we should note the continuance into the fourteenth century of an art-style

[21] It should be noted that the sixteenth-century Reformers did not always destroy the objects they removed from churches. They found it to their advantage to sell these alabasters on a large scale in foreign lands.

[22] The alabasters were always religious or funerary in purpose, however, while the ivory workers turned out many secular pieces, beginning in the fourteenth century.

dominated by a quiet fulness. This was obvious in the choir-enclosure of Notre Dame of Paris, whose carvings are by Jean Ravy and Jean Le Bouteiller; in the destroyed rood-screen of Bourges; in the stone reredo at Fontenay and a nearby Virgin of the same period.

Those fourteenth-century Virgins incline slightly at the hips, looking neither at the Child nor the spectator. Their eyes are fixed before or beyond us in inner contemplation, full of silence and prayer. But already the Virgin at Bayel lowers her eyes towards the little Jesus; a shadow of anxiety beclouds her peace. The church at Écouis has kept a group of ten statues, one of which represents "St Mary the Egyptian" clothed to her feet only in her long hair through which protrude her joined hands.

"At the end of the fourteenth century", Marcel Aubert observed, "two great studios drew all eyes, fixed all trends and proclaimed what the art of the fifteenth century would be". The first was the studio of André Beauneveu of Valenciennes (1330–1403), master-carver and painter of Duke Jean de Berry; Beauneveu was aided and succeeded by Jean of Cambrai, who died in 1438. Both men worked at Bourges and Mehun-sur-Yèvre. The second studio belonged to Claus Sluter (1340–1406), who worked in Dijon at the court of Duke Philip the Bold of Burgundy; in 1389 Sluter became the successor of Jean of Marville. All four of these masters came originally from northern France, Flanders, Hainaut or Holland, like many other artists of the period. For this region, from the late fourteenth century to the sixteenth, was a glorious art center. Tomb-carvers from Tournai, marble-workers, cabinet-makers—all willingly left their homes to go all over Europe, particularly to Burgundy, whose rulers were also their own sovereigns.[23]

[23] In their home region, especially at Antwerp, the carved wooden choir-stalls and large, gilded or painted reredos were outstanding;

The case of Sluter, however, is exceptional. As we examine his statues on the Champmol portal,[24] it seems that a revolution has taken place. The figures stand on jutting consoles, overflowing them with their motion. St Catherine and St John the Baptist present the two princely donors to the Virgin of the *trumeau,* or central pier, with almost declamatory gestures. There is a feeling of air—even of wind—about them. Their draperies are hollowed out in deep folds where shadows gather; the Virgin's garments and the gesture of her right arm make one think already of the seventeenth century. The "Moses Well"—the hexagonal base of a great destroyed calvary—gave the artist and his helper, Claus of Werwe, an opportunity to display all their resources. Six unforgettable prophets here proclaim the Passion. Moses is a powerful, oval figure with a flowing double beard. His garments and those of his companions are hollowed out in massive folds; and their accessories—books, purses and belts—are interpreted with authoritative meticulousness. These statues are the richly accoutred figures of a vast, sacred drama.

Sluter's studio had a tremendous influence. One of its achievements—the tomb of Philip the Bold with its handsome, reclining figures and many small statues of mourners —prepared the way for other magnificent sepulchres.[25]

Yet can this work be interpreted as an example of the "French spirit"? Such vehemence and such a declamatory

---

such works were exported in large quantities, fully carved, all over Europe.

[24] *Translator's note:* A former abbey outside Dijon.

[25] For example, the tomb of Charles I of Bourbon at Souvigny by Jacques Morel, who worked also at Rodez; the tomb of John the Fearless at Dijon by Jean de la Huerta and Antoine Le Moiturier. Tombs with mourners are also found at Lille, for the father-in-law of Philip the Bold, and at Innsbrück for the son-in-law of Charles the Bold.

tendency were not cultivated by French artists. Of course, a prolific, heavy, frankly Flemish realism was current in Picardy.[26] But while the carvers of choir stalls, reredos and tombs in Spain—almost all of whom were foreigners (Flemings, Frenchmen or Germans)—gave themselves over to a kind of wild intoxication and a sumptuous eloquence of detail,[27] the French masterpieces of the late Middle Ages were calm and almost silent. As examples, we have the tomb of Philippe Pot and the "Holy Sepulchres" which Focillon described as *"tableaux vivants in the half-light"*. In spite of the complicated garments worn by the two old men and the strained expressions of the Holy Women of Jerusalem and St John, these late mediaeval works are neither violent nor heart-rending. In the finest representations of "The Entombment of Christ",[28] the face and body of the Victim reveal One who has passed through earthly death to achieve divine peace. The seated figure of Mary Magdalene at Solesmes attains a depth of suffering and quiet prayer expressed with touching reticence by her face, clasped hands and closed lips.

The refined and joyous carvings of Antoine Le Moiturier on the façades of Saint-Antoine and Vienne in the Dauphiné region; the weather-vane in the form of an angel at Le Lude (1475); the forms full of moderation and strength, of health and balance,[29] typical of Michel Colombe (1430–

---

[26] The façade of St Vulfran at Abbeville (1488–1505); the choir enclosure and choir-stalls of the cathedral of Amiens (1490–1531).

[27] Tombs at Burgos and Miraflores; the façade of St Paul's at Valladolid; "the major reredos" at St Nicholas in Burgos; and in the cathedrals of Toledo, Orensa, Oviedo, Seville, and Miraflores (the work of Gil de Siloé).

[28] For example, at the Hospital of Tonnerre by Jean Michel and George de la Sonnette (1455); at Solesmes (1496); at Chaource (1515); or again at Souvigny (in bas-relief).

[29] Here we are concerned with the four cardinal virtues which he erected at the angles of the tomb of the Duke of Brittany in Nantes between 1502 and 1507. We are also indebted to him for the

1512) and his collaborator, Guillaume Regnault;[30] the
sculpture produced in the Champagne and Bourbonnais regions in the early sixteenth century; Ligier Richier's "Crucifixion" in painted stone at Hattonchâtel (1523)[31]—all these
creations are only varied aspects of the *détente,* which, according to Marcel Aubert, overtook French art just prior to
the aesthetic and religious upheavals of the first half of the
sixteenth century.

---

astonishing "St George" formerly in the chapel at Gaillon and now
in the Louvre.

[30] The funerary statue of Robert Legendre, "The Virgin of the
Garden of Olives" (now in the Louvre).

[31] It is important not to reduce the work of this master only to the
macabre and triumphal skeleton at Bar-le-Duc (1547).

CHAPTER VI

ITALY AND THE RENAISSANCE

Now we must return to the distant past in order to follow in Italian sculpture the progress of the revolution known as the Renaissance. If its importance in artistic history is incalculable, its place in religious history is ambiguous. The principal point was a revival of taste for classical antiquity and for antiquity's concepts and forms. These values had never disappeared, especially in Italy. But they subsisted in an over-all atmosphere that had become fully Christian. Now, little by little, the situation was reversed, and a time was to come when the Christian element would seem residual in a broadly pagan art.

The intellectuals discovered in Platonism a means of conciliating man's thrust towards God with the orientation of the whole soul towards that beauty whose priests, heroes and demi-gods are the poets and artists. Michelangelo proclaimed: "Nothing approaches closer to God than the effort to produce a perfect work, since God is perfection." That was a remarkable thought—one completely foreign to the sculptors of Moissac, Chartres or Rheims and to the ecclesiastics who had guided them. Michelangelo affirmed the supreme perfection of God and the sovereign dignity of a work of art, but they are for him of the same nature. The artist—we must remember to use no longer the term "artisan"—is like God a creator (the Platonic demiurge is the connection). Michelangelo spoke of approaching God, whereas a man of the Middle Ages would have spoken of serving God. Both conferred on art a divine mission, but in a radically different context, and the pride each experienced was quite opposite. To sign his work and affirm its beauty meant for the Romanesque sculptor to call down upon it and himself the blessing of God and the prayers of men. For an artist of the Renaissance, the same act meant giving testimony of his ability to produce a "divine work". It did not mean asking for his eternal salvation but attesting and demanding his immortality.

In other words, we see appearing an art-mystique which threatened to ruin the authentically mystical value of beauty and the artist's craft. For it was a kind of idolatry—not exactly the pagan idolatry, which confused the statue made by the hand of man with a god, but a more subtle, haughty and modern form of idolatry—which divinized slightly or greatly the gifts and creative powers of man. Was it not significant to see tombs—especially the tombs made for popes —free themselves of all references to the Gospel? The Christian virtues betray their spiritual meaning to become merely a series of moral allegories or faces of human pride. Certain of them—the purest of all, such as Chastity or that virtue of Humility for which Greek and Latin, the languages of paganism, had no word—disappeared completely, while Strength expressed itself shamelessly in a hundred different ways.

It is extremely difficult to probe the minds and hearts of the Italians of the Renaissance—those pontiffs, princes, prelates, religious, intellectuals, artists and merchants. A double danger lies in wait for us: that of interpreting their acts, works and words, in the light of the conventional mediaeval concept regarded as the norm of Christianity and Christendom, or according to today's perspectives. Currents of almost outspoken paganism and atheism traverse Renaissance Italy (along with a recrudescence of superstitious practices which accommodated themselves well to the new trends. But it would be wrong to imagine there was a collapse of all religious values. To put it briefly, members of the lower and middle classes remained strongly Christian; among cultivated people, however, faith did not remain anchored on God but became steeped in unbaptized waters. Humanists enlarged the area of the sacred—at the risk of confusing it with the superhuman—but what became of sanctity? The saint was regarded as a kind of athlete of the divine through his deeds, whereas the artist became one through his works.

It is interesting to observe that three successive and contradictory movements of purification and "a return to the sources" of religious inspiration denounced, each in its own fashion, the "pagan" vertigo of this artistic splendour: Savonarola's iconoclastic blaze; the Reformation; and the Counter-Reformation. If the first movement was only a temporary episode, the last two have had, as we shall see, great importance for art history, particularly for sculpture. Wherever the Reformation triumphed, it killed sculpture beyond recall. The Counter-Reformation oriented it into channels where it hoped to capture that genial intoxication the Renaissance had caused to overflow on all sides and put it to work for the greater glory of God—by dint of that "presiding eloquence and *caeli caelorum*", as St Vincent de Paul used to say about a certain sacred eloquence current in his day.

*   *   *

Frederick II of Hohenstauffen (1194–1250), the Holy Roman Emperor who was a great adversary of the papacy and an equally great admirer of the ancient and Arabic philosophers, was a curious figure for the middle of the thirteenth century. He was far behind his day in his apparent desire to revive a Constantinian era; yet he was far ahead of his day in his many qualities that were already those of a princely Maecenas, a freethinker and one anxious to arrange political and moral actions to the benefit of earthly profits and glories. In the areas of southern Italy over which he ruled, he developed a monumental art full of secular pride after the manner of the ancient Romans. He erected at Capua a triumphal arch on which he was shown in a toga, surrounded by statues of his ministers. A famous bust of a woman adorns the pulpit at Ravello. Does it represent the donor? The Church? One thing about it is certain: That head of a matron wearing a diadem is without any Christian *aura* and makes us think of either a Roman goddess or an empress.

Frederick II's movement was ephemeral but significant. Nicola Pisano, who produced in 1260 the pulpit at Pisa as the first masterpiece of a new art, was acquainted with the sculpture of Apulia and Campania inspired by Frederick II. Nicola was obviously inspired also by the art of the sarcophagi. Beginning with that time, the taste and influence of antiquity would constantly increase, reaching their apogee in sixteenth-century Rome when the popes zealously encouraged the excavations that brought to light the "Laocoön", "Niobe's Children" and the "Farnese Hercules", and swarms of sculptors, dazzled by the magic spell of these works, indefatigably copied and restored them.

It would obviously be absurd to try to connect everything during those three centuries of Italian sculpture to the supremacy of ancient models in art style. Many works—some of them among the purest, most charming and most Christian ever produced, such as the Sienese statues of painted wood—owed little or nothing to this taste. But this was what dictated boldness to the Pisan or Florentine artists of the late thirteenth and early fourteenth centuries; this was what dominated their method of treating draperies, poses and faces; and this was what oriented sculptors towards monumental works—the heroic nude, the equestrian figure or the colossal.

The five panels of Pisa Cathedral's pulpit are resolutely in the ancient style. In the "Adoration of the Magi", for example, the full beards, robust necks, heavy figures, amply draped garments, and heads of three horses with manes stirred by the wind are quite Roman. The orderly arrangement of the figures in depth as well as the impression of foreshortening, although still clumsy, are other signs of the wish to renew ties to antiquity.

Curiously enough, seven years later, when Nicola worked with his son Giovanni and Arnolfo di Cambio on the relief sculpture of Siena Cathedral's pulpit, he produced a work more "French" in feeling. As at Pisa, we find scenes from the life of Christ, including the Crucifixion and Last Judgement, but less oratorical and academic in style. The modelling is more quivering, more nervous—and less muscular. Nothing is more curious than the translation of French themes by the chisel of a marble worker imbued with the ancient nobility but still profoundly sensitive to Christian grace: the prophets, virtues and liberal arts. Among the countless subjects of the fountain in Perugia (1278) were the signs of the Zodiac and the labours of the months. But the dominant French inspiration does not prevent us from discovering here also the she-wolf of Rome with her sucklings and a personification of Rome, the "capital of the world".

The early fourteenth-century pulpits of Pistoia and Pisa cathedrals are the works of Giovanni alone. Hollowing out deeply the shadows, emphasizing and multiplying volume, attitudes and feelings, those works constitute excessively laden relief tableaux. At Pisa, Hercules and St Michael can be seen as caryatids sharing symbolically the burden of power. The four cardinal virtues support a crowned figure representing the city of Pisa, while an image of the standing Christ is accompanied by the four Evangelists. (Hercules is shown in the nude, and, somewhat unexpectedly, so also is the virtue of Prudence.) Nowhere else in Italy can one find this close association of pagan, civic and Christian themes. Giovanni Pisano's Virgins are firmly, even harshly, Roman with their straight noses and heavy chins, although their over-all attitude is like that of our Gothic Virgins.

We do not have space here to study the work of Arnolfo di Cambio at Rome (which was condemned to an artistic eclipse, in any case, as a result of the popes' removal to Avignon). And also we do not have space to consider the work of Tino di Camaino at Florence and Naples. But we should point out the achievements of two Sienese artists, Ramo di Paganello, whose connection to France is estab-lished, and Lorenzo Maitani. Enzo Carli[1] has revealed them as the creators of the admirable relief panels on the façade of Orvieto cathedral.

The four Orvieto panels form a quiet, noble design, full of great delicacy of detail; they are dedicated to scenes from the Book of Genesis, the Tree of Jesse, the Life of Christ and the Last Judgement. The work is characterized by an airy composition, which lets wide sections of the background show through. In scenes of the Creation and Fall of Man, a young, loving God gives life to Adam and Eve and warns them before He punishes them, under the eyes of the angels, who at first are admiring and affectionate and later sorrow-ful. Our first parents are supple nudes who do not need to seem "modest" in order to be chaste.

This work might be the masterpiece of Italian Christian sculpture, if we did not have in addition—also by Maitani or anonymous Sienese disciples of his—unforgettable statues of polychrome wood: images of Christ on the Cross and the Virgin. Especially noteworthy are the carvings of an An-nunciation scene; Gabriel is wingless, and Mary stands in a long garment with quiet folds. Each faces the other in a kind of mutual obedience that is dignified, mute, attentive and almost fraternal. Both are perfect servants and perfect mes-sengers of grace.

Andrea da Pontedera, known as Pisano (1270–1348),

[1] *La Sculpture siennoise en bois,* Milan and Florence, 1954.

was the first great Florentine master. He cast in bronze the
doors of Florence's baptistry (1330), which contain twenty
panels relating episodes in the life of St John the Baptist.
For Florence Cathedral's bell-tower he also cast fifty-four
medallions in the shape of diamonds and hexagons. His art
has a serene sobriety; it is sweet but not dainty, and it em-
ploys few figures, as is the case with the Orvieto reliefs
which, indeed, have sometimes been attributed to him and his
son Nino.

In Andrea's work, we see mythological scenes, for example, Daedalus trying on his wings, side by side with episodes from the Book of Genesis and allegories of the seven
Virtues and seven Sciences. It is noteworthy as a complete
gallery of all of Florence's arts and crafts. This achievement
is as interesting for our understanding of the history of man's
technical progress as for the forms that charm our eye. We
see not only the labours of the field as symbols of the passage of time but also as connected somewhat remotely to
the conditions imposed on all the sons of Adam by the Fall.
All man's activities are shown with due prominence for
artists, such as the musician, architect, painter and sculptor
(the last named is carving the statuette of a nude youth);
also shown are soldiers, monks, merchants and magistrates.
We have an exact picture, in well-ordered variety and pros-
perity, of daily life in a civilization that is mainly urban,
industrial and intent on trade. The accuracy of Andrea's
bird's-eye view and the delicacy of his chisel have made
each of these small scenes a masterpiece on a par with the
Amiens medallions of the previous century. Despite the
representation of the seven sacraments and the Christian
virtues, the general feeling of the work is secular. This is,
indeed, the city of men. When Florence traced this noble,
sound and attractive self-portrait, she offered it to herself, it
seems, rather than to God.[2]

[2] Andrea da Pontedera carved these bas-reliefs after the designs

At Verona, the studio of the Campionesi family carved tombs for the Scaliger dynasty that are monuments of princely pride. Placed under the open sky in the heart of the city, they are typified by the equestrian statue of the ruler, Can Grande della Scala, who is in full battle array. While there are religious subjects among the other decorative bas-reliefs, such figures fail to confer a Christian significance on the tombs. The same judgement may be made on the strange biblical, mythological, allegorical and narrative conglomeration we find among the exterior carvings of Venice's ducal palace.

*   *   *

Florence dominated completely the sculpture of the Quattrocento.[3] The famous competition of 1401 over the adornment of the baptistry's second pair of doors was a departure-point of an extraordinary flowering. The commission was entrusted to Lorenzo Ghiberti (1378–1455), an artist known only as a bronze-caster. He worked twenty years on the twenty New Testament scenes and eight figures of the Evangelists and Doctors of the West which comprise that composition. Immediately afterwards and for more than another two decades, he devoted himself to the ten panels of the third pair

---

of Giotto, whom he had succeeded as architect of the bell-tower. Andrea Orcagna was an architect, painter, goldsmith and sculptor (the tabernacle of Or San Michele, for example, is his work). In such men we see the astonishing multiplicity of skills and talents distinguishing so many geniuses of the Italian Renaissance. Worth noting also is the importance of their studio training. Orcagna was Giotto's pupil. Nino Pisano, son of Andrea da Pontedera, was a great sculptor. In no way was his art inferior to his father's. Nino's best works are free-standing statues, including Madonnas and representations of "The Annunciation". One of his achievements is a "Pietà", a subject more rare in Italian sculpture than might be believed.

[3] Jacopo della Quercia (1371–1438) of Sienna was the only master not from Florence. We are indebted to him for the bas-reliefs of San Petronio in Bologna, which reveal a solemn, sober strength, not at all inclined to prettiness of detail.

of doors, which are known as the "Gates of Paradise" because they retrace episodes from the Book of Genesis. With rare felicity Ghiberti's art joins the charm of detail to the gift of completing and giving rhythmic accents to a composition without overburdening it.

In the "Gates of Paradise" Ghiberti created several planes, row on row, as in an easel painting; he conveyed an impression of depth at the same time by reducing the size of the background figures and progressively diminishing the size of their relief until they were only a kind of outline engraved on bronze; by contrast, the figures closest to the spectator are almost in the round.

The organization of the many angels and human figures, of trees in the Garden of Eden, and of architectural elements is handled with calculated skill. A virtuosity is revealed in the use of resources (without becoming intoxicated by them); everything is treated with a "Florentine" kind of grace—airy, pure and youthful in feeling. The difficult art of rendering a "sculptured landscape" has never been practised with such mastery. And when the artist scatters lizards and blossoms on the ground as well as birds in the branches of an oak-tree, olive-tree or nut-tree, he does it with premeditated affection— full of freshness yet without naïveté—for the inexhaustible treasures Nature offers anyone knowing how to observe her.

In this same period the nine-foot statues of John the Baptist, St. Matthew and St Stephen on Or San Michele, and also the Portal of the Oval sculptured by Nanni de Banco on the cathedral represent a step forward towards a monumental and classical kind of eloquence.

Donatello (1386–1466) was the master of a whole school of sculpture. His work embraces all forms of the art: statues in the round, high relief and bas-relief, bronze, marble, wood and even terra cotta; and his subjects include Madonnas, prophets, saints, angels, laymen and equestrian figures. The keyboard of his sensitivity is as broad as his technical skill.

He could fix in marble a feeling of delightful tenderness as in the "Madonna dei Pazzi".[4] His "St George" is the image of strength and rectitude, even if shown with a frown on his forehead. And the bronze portrait of a young bishop—Louis of Toulouse—radiates grace not only through the hand raised in benediction but also through the ideally peaceful countenance. St John the Baptist as a child provides an opportunity to carve the bust of a ten-year-old boy, but the artist also suggests the desert penitent by giving to the figure an emaciated, fierce look.

In fact, Donatello's inclination was towards impetuosity, drama and violence. To experience this we have but to compare his marble "Jeremiah" to Ghiberti's "St Matthew": Both are orators dressed in togas, but their methods of conducting themselves and their expressions are quite different. The "David" and "Judith" cast as adornments for the garden of the Medici palace are heroic bronzes; yet despite their subject-matter they convey no religious impression.

Among Donatello's other great works are the "Christ on the Cross" and "Deposition from the Cross" of Padua; the "Pietà" of San Lorenzo's in Florence (in which Mary's profile under her veil seems even more ghastly than her Son's); and the famous "Mary Magdalene" (which Charles de Brosses has described in these words: "She is so dry, blackened, disheveled and frightful that she has discouraged me forever from any thought of penance").

All these works are impressive masterpieces, but it seems that the artist has used the sorrowful mysteries of Christianity to achieve an exaggerated expression of his talent for portraying pathos—at least as much as he has used pathos in the service of religious meditation.

Two comments are required with respect to Donatello and the art trend that began with his work. First, we behold in

---

[4] Now in the Berlin museum; a great many relief works in painted stucco or terra cotta are derived from this work.

him an extraordinary generalization—if not a vulgarization—
of technical skill. The least of the minor Florentine masters
is capable of making honourable, and even quite lovely, re-
sponses to the fashionable themes of the day. Thus the
medallion of the "Madonna and Child" by Desiderio da
Settignano (1428–1464) in Santa Croce at Florence was a
prototype for countless Madonnas by Rossellino, Mino da
Fiesole and many other artists. Like skilled practitioners,
they had so well mastered this subject-matter that they could
apply it almost without change to statues of "Charity"; and
if Charity holds only one *putto,* instead of the two with whom
she is generally shown, she seems like just another Madonna.

Secondly, the almost mechanical exploitation of maternal
and childish grace is a tiresome aspect of Florentine sculpture. As an example, let us mention the enamelled terra
cottas produced for more than a century by the heirs of Lucca
della Robbia; also—on the façade of San Bernadino at Perugia—the cabochons depicting cherubs' heads against a
background of wings which Agostino di Duccio used to cover
vast surfaces in a monotonous variety. Along with the cherubs'
heads he also employed angel-musicians—fiery, spark-like
figures apparently swirling in the wind.

Next, a contamination of sculpture by painting can be observed. This is the great era of bas-reliefs. Lucca della
Robbia (1400–1482) produced no statues in the round at all,
and his nephew Andrea (1435–1525) very few.[5] The della
Robbias succeeded in a new technique of glazed polychrome
terra cotta; their sober colours consisted chiefly of whites and
blues. When they used this technique to decorate monuments
such as Florence's Foundling Hospital or Santa Maria della
Quercia at Viterbo, their "lunettes"—despite an impression

[5] Let us note, however, the "Visitation" group at Pistoia, in which
Mary—a girl of fifteen—bows to Elizabeth, a sixty-year-old woman
full of wrinkles who kneels before Mary. As for Verrocchio, he
directly imitated his master Donatello in the famous "David" of
the Bargello.

of relief—recall not so much a north European tympanum as some kind of pictorial ornamentation. Andrea della Robbia even produced true triptyches, including a *predella* and framework.

Benedetto da Maiano, who is noted for his panels on the life of St Francis in Santa Croce, and Antonio Pollaiuolo both transposed directly into marble or bronze the effects of paintings. In all of this we note a definite decline of sculptural feeling. This is all the more obvious since, at the same time, the increase in technical skill, the fondness for ancient models, the taste for luxury and artistic "collections" had led to an extraordinary development of the minor arts, such as diminutive bronzes, the works of goldsmiths and silversmiths, medals and cameos.

The sixteenth century was dominated by the immense personality of Michelangelo (1475–1564).

It is worth interjecting here that Leonardo da Vinci, who tried everything, was also a sculptor, but different statements of his show that painting was far more important, in his eyes, than sculpture. He considered the former to be more intellectual and spiritual than the latter, which was carried out in sweat, dust and disorder: Works of sculpture are doubtless more durable, but they are paralyzed in the intimate expression of poetry and the refined shadings of light. "Sculptors cannot represent transparent bodies, reflexions, surfaces sparkling like mirrors, fog or overcast weather," he said, and added: "I know how to judge such matters since I practise both arts to the same degree." [6] Whatever the case may be, no work of sculpture has survived that can be attributed with certainty to Leonardo.

Michelangelo, on the other hand, was first of all and basi-

[6] Cited by A. Vallentin in *Leonard de Vinci,* p. 217. It is to be noted that Romanesque artists and, in quite a different way, Baroque artists did not hesitate to carve clouds and the rays of the sun or of divine grace.

cally a sculptor. He conceived of sculpture in an essentially
"agonistic" fashion. The problem was to remove from the
inert mass the concept hidden within it[7] which genius liberated with great effort. Hence the symbolic meaning we are
permitted to give to so many striking aspects of his career.
He worked alone, struggling like an athlete against the rebellious yet docile inertia of the marble. His colossal "David"
was to a degree "dictated" to him by an enormous, unused
block of marble whose challenge he was determined to accept. The first work attributed to him with certainty is a
tumultuous "Battle of the Centaurs" in which he interpreted
what he had learned from a passionate study of the ancient
works and lessons in anatomy. The unfinished state of the
four "Slaves" at Florence, of "Day", the "Rondanini Pietà"
and the "Pietàs" at Palestrina and Florence[8] is the sign of a
kind of triumphal failure of his will to conquer his materials.

There is no space here for us to take up, after so many
other commentators, the study of Michelangelo's intimate
drama, the aspects that were heroic, despairing, tremendous
and eternally grandiose in the "testimony" he has left us. But
we are concerned with the question of how his work can
be considered Christian. When he conceived of the tomb of
Julius II, Michelangelo "saw" several dozen gigantic figures
on it, but he completed only the famous "Moses", which is
now in San Pietro in Vincoli.[9] For the Medici Chapel he
created, in addition to the effigies of Lorenzo and Giuliano
de' Medici, the allegorical figures of "Day", "Night", "Dawn"

---

[7] "The outstanding artist has no concept at all which the marble
does not already contain within itself." (Quoted by Fred Berence,
Michel-Ange, p. 507.)

[8] The last-named "Pietà" at Florence was broken by the master
in a fit of violent despair. It was later repaired by Michelangelo's
pupil Calcagni, who added the unfortunate female figure on the
left of the main group.

[9] The "Rachel" and "Lia" that accompany the "Moses" are of a
much later date and cannot be considered to be by Michelangelo's
hand.

and "Twilight" as well as the "Medici Madonna". Moses, the
lawgiver of the Hebrews,[10] is an affirmation of superhuman
energy, or unshakeable power—a muscular colossus seated
with all the force of his full weight, a figure of irresistible
majesty with his haughty glance, barbed horns and tremendous beard. He is the River Nile or an Olympian old
man. But he is not a prophet because he announces nothing
and no one. He is defiant, attentive and silent. All his
strength can do nothing either for the glory of God or the
salvation of men.

Michelangelo's Madonnas do not have the athletic character of the Sistine Chapel sibyls, but he has given them a
kind of virile, morose nobility which alienates them from us.
The chubby Child that turns towards the "Medici Madonna",
or learns to read at the knees of the "Pitti Madonna", we
feel, is not interested in His mother, whose glance is fixed in
abstract meditation. The theme of the "Pietà", so dear to
Michelangelo's sombre genius, is the one that carries the
burden of his truly religious sense of the tragic.

Michelangelo's first "Pietà" (1499)—the one in St Peter's
in Rome—is also the most peaceful of them all. Over a
Christ whose body is as fair as Endymion's, the refined
countenance of His mother is inclined. She seems younger
than her Son, and her face is softened by the veil that frames
it. The "Pietà" in the Duomo of Florence was executed fifty
years later. The artist, who was no longer in torment, intended it as his own funerary monument: This pyramidal
group is dominated by the form of Nicodemus, who wears a
costume vaguely like a monk's habit; he is believed to
represent Michelangelo himself. The whole mood is set by
the prostrate body of Christ, which forms a sinking, zigzag
pattern. The Palestrina "Pietà" (identified only in our century

---

[10] The "Moses" is badly served, to speak frankly, by its present
location. It was to have faced a statue of St Paul, which was never
executed.

as a work of Michelangelo) is more vertical in construction;
Mary scarcely appears at all behind the emaciated body of
Christ, whose shoulders she supports. The fainting Magdalene clings to the group at the right. The "Rondanini Madonna" also had a figure of the Magdalene at one time but
it has been removed (only one of her arms has survived), and,
in its tragically unfinished state, the group sacrifices everything to a vertical feeling that seems inappropriate to the
subject.

Paradoxically, during the last months of his life, Michelangelo—the great poet of physical strength—used straight
lines to depict the prostration and grief of the death of God;
in the artist's last "Pietà", Christ's legs are scarcely bent,
and the two bodies of the group are so narrow that we cannot see where their arms might have been. Thus did Michelangelo depict, through the agonizing appeal of death, the
invincible appeal of the life to come.

*   *   *

There was no connection, however, between Michelangelo's countenance of genius and the swarm of satellite
sculptors he eclipsed with his brilliance—artists like Andrea
Sansovino (1460–1529), who worked in Venice, and his
pupil Jacopo (1486–1570), who even adopted Andrea's
surname; or men like Cattaneo, Baccio Bandinelli and Bar-
tolomeo Ammannati. They shared a common fondness for
nude figures and heroic achievements. Their favourite works
were monumental tombs and fountains of even more monumental proportions. Luxuriantly glistening statues of tritons
and water nymphs reigned on the fountains, while allegorical
virtues announced their grief and majesty on the tombs. That
art, which seemed to have as its sole purpose the desire to
create an impact, swept irresistibly across all Europe.

King René brought the first Italian artists to France about

the middle of the fifteenth century.[11] Next, Louis XII summoned Guido Mazzini to carve the royal tomb. Antonio della Porta also was active in France, and the Justs, a Florentine dynasty of artists, flourished at Tours between 1500 and 1530. During the sixteenth century, the Italian peninsula became the land of great art *par excellence* for rulers in all parts of Europe. The Italian masters—even artists of mediocre talents—profited by this fashion and emigrated in great numbers. Under Francis I, France was deluged by them; the outstanding artists of this group were Francesco Primaticcio and Domenico the Florentine, who carved, for example, the handsome, yet weary, nude athlete known as "Christ at the Pillar" in St Nicholas' Church in Troyes.

French sculptors were strongly influenced by the prestige of Italian art. Ligier Richier doubtless remained most faithful to the French tradition, but Jean Goujon, Pierre Bontemps and Germain Pilon—the last-named was Catherine de' Medici's favourite sculptor—all deliberately imitated the Italian style. In their works, pagan themes, such as nymphs, graces and Dianas, mingled with allegorical subjects to form a curious domain—one that was to be cultivated increasingly —jointly held by paganism and Christianity. Among the favourite subjects were Fame and the Virtues. We should mention among works in this style the old rood-screen in the church of St Germain l'Auxerrois by Goujon; the Louvre has preserved its statues of the Evangelists and "The Burial of Christ". And we have Pilon's "Virgin of Mercy" (1586) as well as his St Francis kneeling in ecstasy, which seems already to exalt the artistic formulas of the Counter-Reformation.[12]

There is no doubt that tomb sculpture provided the best

---

[11] Notably Francesco Laurana, the sculptor of the "Carrying of the Cross" in St Didier's church at Avignon (1478).
[12] This work is in the church of St John and St Francis in Paris.

opportunity to make an impact. For, in accord with the artist's need, it permitted a triumphal display of noble idealism, the harsh truth of portraiture or the assumption of elegantly languid poses by reclining statues of the dead. The Christian significance of such works appears especially through the power of allusion, as in the theme of the "praying figure" which is shown kneeling and with clasped hands. The finest example of this kind of sculpture is the portrait of Chancellor de Birague by Germain Pilon.[13]

In Spain, the Italian influence came into play in a slightly different way. Sansovino, Moreto, Fancelli and Pietro Torrigiano worked in Spain between 1490 and 1530. On the other hand, some Spaniards went to Italy for their art training; among them were Bartolomé Ordonez and Michelangelo's disciple Alonso Berruguete, who died in 1561. If we also note that certain Italians, like Bigarny or Leone Leoni, became "Hispanicized" to a great extent and that many French artists under the influence of the Italian style[14] went to work in Spain and Portugal, then we shall understand the great complexity of the situation.

The achievement of an artist like Damian Forment is an eloquent testimony of this complexity. He carved ornaments and figures for the prows of ships—religious sculpture without a doubt, since the fleet of the Catholic kings was under the full protection of God, the Virgin and the saints. But his speciality was carving reredos of wood or alabaster (for example, in the monastery of Poblet and the cathedral of Huesca), and he sometimes employed the Gothic style and at other times the Italian style. One of Forment's most Spanish characteristics is the proliferation of his art; the adornment is total in nature. Sculpture invades the whole structure, covering from top to bottom the major chapel

[13] This work, dating from 1584, is in the Louvre.
[14] For example, the pulpit in Santa Cruz at Coimbra, 1522.

like a vine on a wall. His reredos consist of five or six storeys, superimposed one on top of the other, and multiplying panels, niches and framework. The spectator's eye wanders, leaps and flits over holy scenes and saintly figures. Many other artists turned out quantities of reredos that compete with Forment's in their gigantic size and tumult; among them was Juan Rodriguez who worked at El Parral near Segovia.

If viewed close up—to the extent that this is possible—such art is obviously fond of violent impressions. The fragments of the reredo of San Benito, now in the museum of Valladolid, offer an opportunity to examine Berruguete's style. It consists of elongated human forms; twisted, flame-like patterns; and exaggerated poses. The same artist carved for the cathedral of Toledo a huge "Transfiguration of Christ" which seems agitated by the ocean waves. Standing before it, we feel a desire to murmur the old prayer: *"Non in commotione, Dominus. . . ."*

Sixteenth-century Spanish sculpture is noisy and indiscreet. It is full of pride—the pride of the artist and the pride of the great of this world, as reflected in their tomb carvings.[15] But one thing is certain: The sensually pagan aspect of Italian art was never introduced into it. Spanish sculpture instinctively rejected the nude. There was almost a spontaneous censorship in this development which was in a way a foretaste of the Counter-Reformation. White marble—the material especially suited for the nude—never really conquered Spain, which has always preferred polychromed wood. Thus the transition from Gothic to Renaissance style and from Renaissance to Baroque took place in Spain (where all

---

[15] The tombs of Cardinal Ximenes de Cisneros, at Alcalà de Henarès; of Philip the Handsome and Joanna the Mad, at Grenada, the work of Ordonez; and of Cardinal de Tavera, at Toledo, the work of Berruguete.

three styles assumed exalted forms) without the direct intrusions of subjects like the Hercules and Galateas which invaded Christian sculpture elsewhere.

England also welcomed Italian sculptors, especially the same Torrigiano whom we have already mentioned for his work in Spain. It was in Spain, indeed, that he died. Torrigiano's principal claim to fame was that, as a youth in Florence, he had smashed with his fist the nose of a fellow apprentice, Michelangelo. In like manner, the destiny of English sculpture was to be smashed by the Protestant Reformation.

CHAPTER VII

THE REFORMATION AND THE AGE OF THE BAROQUE

All in all, the Reformation was resolutely iconoclastic. Doubtless we can find some statements by Luther, and even by Calvin, disavowing the violent acts of their disciples. But it is clear that the spirit of their teachings was deeply hostile to images. Zwingli showed no regret in 1529 as he stood in the cathedral of Bern before a heap of art-works sacked during a riot and announced: "If our behaviour harmed the saints in heaven, and if they had the power attributed to them, could you have really cut off their arms and heads?" [1]

The arguments of the Byzantine controversy over the images were repeated: Every image which seeks to represent God and causes him to be adored under material forms is tainted with idolatry and sacrilege. Christ is present in the Church through His living Word, and for this reason the temple shelters the Bible. If absolutely necessary, a bare wooden cross may recall His sacrifice, but under no circumstances should there be an image of Christ, "for there is no

[1] Quoted by P. Romane-Musculus. *La prière des mains*, Geneva. 1938. This little book is a useful summary of Protestant attitudes towards art problems.

image more in danger of being served and adored than His".
(If the saints were removed, it was because superstition had
endowed their images with absurd powers, but theoretically
images of the saints could have been retained as mere witnesses.) Thus the favourite themes of late mediaeval iconography—"Christ on the Cross", the "Trinity", the "Madonna and Child", and the "Pietà" are worthy of condemna-
tion by their very nature.

As a result, we have a development which at first seems
paradoxical but only corroborates what had taken place previously at Byzantium: It is not the pagan or neutral works
that incur the wrath of the Reformers. This explains why
the greatest French sculptors of the sixteenth century could
be Huguenots. Ligier Richier, Jean Goujon and Pierre Bontemps all went into exile either voluntarily or of necessity
after 1562, when the religious wars began in France. It may
be presumed that Goujon experienced more pangs of conscience in carving the "Burial of Christ" than when he
worked on the nymphs in his famous "Fountain of the Inno-
cents". Barthélemy Prieur decorated palaces and tombs with
strictly secular and allegorical subjects. The result of that
great movement of "returning to the Christian sources",
which the Reformation claimed to be, was a sterilization of
Christian sculpture. There was no Protestant sculpture, and
there could be none; at the most, we have a few works by
Protestant artists—which is not the same thing. In any case,
what choice was there between Jean Goujon and Marcel
Gimond?

Of course, religious art of the late Middle Ages and
Renaissance had entered dangerous paths. The most extravagant growths were smothering the tree of the true faith;
souls and works of art alike were fed on a host of legends
and superstitions which kept the faithful outrageously well
informed about a hundred degenerate forms of the divine
and removed them from knowledge of authentic truth. In

order to fight Huguenot propaganda and at the same time
do justice to what enlightened minds felt was legitimate in
the Huguenot position, there was a tendency, beginning in
the middle of the sixteenth century, to subject sacred subjects to narrow restrictions. All the ceremonies of Henri II's
entrance into Paris in 1549 were conducted in the ancient
classical style; it is interesting to note that Jean Goujon and
J. Cousin were among those who arranged these ceremonies.
There were no *tableaux vivants* or religious scenes "in order
to avoid the juggling acts formerly associated with such
events".

There was a fearful destruction of "Papist" idols in the
lands of the Reformers. The first iconoclastic wave swept
over England between 1548 and 1550, bringing the elimina-
tion of images as "corrupt, vain and superstitious". Special
targets of attack were the great wooden statues of Christ on
the Cross between the Virgin and St John which were on the
beam of glory in most churches. We have records of pay-
ments to the teams officially responsible for knocking down
such images and burning them. Crosses in cemeteries were
levelled, reredos and altars destroyed.

In the next century, in 1640, the Puritans of the Long
Parliament renewed the destructive acts, sending commit-
tees of purification to inspect the churches. A certain William Downsing has left a diary in which he relates his exploits: He congratulates himself before God and men because, with the help of the "faithful"—let us understand
here that he is referring to a horde of fanatics—he "cleansed"
eleven churches at Ipswich in a single day. A priest named
Richard Culmer boasts that at Canterbury he has "tumbled
down head first" the statues of Christ and the twelve apostles. Here and there, tombs were sacked, not so much for
religious reasons as out of cupidity—to lay hands on precious
objects that might have been buried with prelates.[2]

[2] In fact, funerary carvings were the only ones preserved, and

In France, the upheavals of 1562, in particular, unleashed acts of violence, and the total destruction was frightful.[3] These are the saddest of all the forms of vandalism religious sculpture has had to endure. Although ordinary hooliganism and blind hatred were involved, the destruction was carried out in the name of the Christian faith on Christian works. It is a dreadful scandal to see a testimony of purity clash violently with a testimony of beauty.

*   *   *

Christian sculpture was henceforth limited to Catholic countries: Italy, France, Spain, Flanders, certain Swiss cantons, southern Germany and Austria. But it developed, because of the Reformation, quite differently from the sculpture of the Middle Ages and Renaissance. It was the art of the Counter-Reformation.

The Catholic Church felt in many ways vulnerable to the Reformers' criticism. Under their pressure, although she still vigorously maintained the legitimacy and holiness of religious art, the Church undertook a strict examination of conscience. This was all the more the case since sarcastic remarks and reprimands were received not only from rebellious Christians but also from humanists like Erasmus and almost all the other enlightened men who had remained within the bosom of Catholicism.

---

the only kind that continued to be practiced in England as well as Holland (for example, at Rombaut and Verhulst). England has preserved about two thousand tombs of the later Middle Ages. Various waves of vandalism in France, especially that of the sans-culottes, decimated the French monuments of this sort.

[3] We can gain an idea of this in L. Réau's *Monuments detruits de l'art français,* Vol. I, pp. 65–106. We ought to include—although this does not in any way correct the damage—cases of vandalism against the Huguenots, such as the one mentioned by P. Romane-Musculus, *op. cit.* Some works of sculpture by Ligier Richier were buried in the seventeenth century by a bishop of Verdun who did not want to preserve the works of a Calvinistic artist.

In France, such critics expressed the following desire in the Articles of Poissy (1561):

> . . . that parish priests should carefully and frequently warn their parishioners not to think there is any divinity or particular powers in any image. . . . Let them correct everything painted, carved or moulded that is evil, false, ridiculous or dishonourable.

The same critics decreed in 1563 at the Council of Trent as follows:

> No images shall be exposed to veneration which might lead to false teaching or give an opportunity for simple persons to fall into error. . . . No profane or affected embellishments or additions shall be used. . . . No image shall be set up without the approval of the bishop . . .

In 1568, the Flemish theologian Molanus wrote a detailed treatise which deduced the consequences of such precepts. Some of his statements were aimed at mediaeval traditions, others at aberrations due to the paganising taste of the period.

The apochryphal Gospels and the Golden Legend were strictly outlawed. Many charming subjects and a host of popular saints disappeared. People suddenly regarded as ridiculous, sacrilegious and naïve—to use a word which will not admit of any excuse for the three hundred years to come —such subjects as St Christopher the good giant; St Antony and his pig; or God the Father and His tiara. Some naïvetés were attacked only as silly or irreverent; others for theological reasons, too, as was the case with representations of the Trinity in the form of three similar human figures, or of the Word descending on Mary in the form of a naked baby riding a ray of grace.

The dead Christ had inspired countless pathetic works focussing on the Virgin's grief. Suddenly, such subjects were regarded as suspect, for the Gospel had said nothing about Mary's presence or, for obvious reasons, about her desperate grief as her Son's body was prepared for burial. Henceforth, we shall no longer see Christ's Mother weeping over His body, or God the Father holding His Son on His knees in order to offer men the tragic proof of their redemption's price.

Cabinet-makers in the French and Flemish tradition had formerly decorated church stalls with a host of leering forms inspired by the *fabliaux* and popular sayings, or by the artisan's own lively spirits. There was nothing edifying about such works, of course, but neither the faithful nor the canons thought such bits of mischief were inspired by the Evil One. But the new spirit of sobriety no longer tolerated these subjects in church, where people were supposed to feel themselves in the house of God—not "at home".

"The Marital Spanking" was not thought to inspire "guilty thoughts". But the same judgement could not be made about nude figures that were too flexible or too muscular. In 1560, Pilon carved a famous group—the "Three Graces", whose short garments revealed rather than concealed their forms. Of course, there was nothing funereal about the work, although it was designed to shelter Henri II's heart. When Catherine de' Medici decided to place it in the monastery of the Celestines, the Graces were baptized as the theological Virtues. Before long, however, such subterfuges would no longer be possible.[4] Chastity became the order of the day. In 1581 Ammannati solemnly disavowed his excessively voluptuous works in these words: "Not being able to destroy my figures, I wish to say to all who see them that I regret making them." And it was possible to witness the "covering up"

---

[4] It goes without saying that the nude had great prominence in profane decorations. The child-like nude cherub continued to caper in all corners of sacred sculpture, provided it remained chaste. This offered a splendid opportunity for artists to display contorted figures. On the other hand, an allegorical interpretation might lend itself to all kinds of complacencies. For example, Cardinal Berberini, the future pope, wittily discovered in Bernini's statue "Daphnis" a warning against the temptations of sensual love.

—this seems the correct expression—of overly daring works; sometimes they might even be destroyed.

Thus important changes in orientation were noted. A concern for critical severity, dignity and austerity quite legitimately sought to regenerate religious art in accord with the needs of theology, morality and artistic taste. For this reason, we should be greatly in error—as Émile Mâle has shown—if we imagined Christian art had ceased to exist. The fact remains that, to grasp its grandeur and scope, we must break completely with the aesthetic and spiritual perspectives of the Middle Ages. The prelates and artists of the seventeenth and eighteenth centuries did not find this difficult at all. Their writings and deeds showed the total scorn they felt for the "Gothic" period, whose barbarism was so obvious that no discussion was needed. L. Réau points out that, in 1765, a certain Abbé Laugier, who congratulated himself over the recent disappearance from Amiens cathedral of "the horrible rood-screen and coarse, monstrous altar", wanted also to get rid of the choir-stalls, which he described as a "mass of crude knick-knacks". In 1789, the Bishop of Limoges preserved from the destruction of his cathedral's rood-screen only the carvings of the "Labours of Hercules"—a remarkable paradox, which seemed quite natural at the time.

We men of today—whom the Romantic reaction has accustomed to a feeling of admiration for the Middle Ages—are faced with a quite different temptation: the desire to fix forever our criterion of the Christian spirit in a golden age that was both conventional and confused, since it extended from the twelfth century to the fifteenth. But if our taste acquires a flexibility and tolerance, we should be able to escape the dilemma of being forced to condemn either Gislebert or Bernini.

For that purpose, however, we must do away with certain misunderstandings and clarify certain ambiguities. If no one dares any longer reproach the Middle Ages for their "clumsiness" and "ignorance", the violence and technical excesses of the Baroque suffice, in the minds of many, to condemn this style. Yet we must object to this argument by pointing out that the Middle Ages also knew wild excesses of technical proficiency. And if we examine more closely what is included under such labels as "the Jesuit style", "Baroque and rococo", or "classic" and "academic", we shall see the formation of differences and even marked contrasts which prevent us from encompassing everything in sweeping judgements.

The sculpture of the seventeenth and eighteenth centuries was well organized for the glory of God—in fact, far more solidly than had been the case in the sixteenth century. Such adornment was intended to be official, militant and radiant. Bernini was an ardent Christian, deeply nourished by the spirituality of St Ignatius of Loyola. In Italy, Flanders and, for even stronger reasons, in Spain, artists were truly sons of the Church; not infrequently, they were themselves churchmen.

How does it happen, then, that their works fail to convince us of their faith? Because—if we may use a comparison drawn from the world of music, a soloist in a sacred oratorio convinces us only with difficulty of the sincerity of her role—even if, in fact especially if, she puts her whole soul into her singing. The audience is not inclined to consider her performance from the standpoint of sincerity. And this is what happens in this new form of Christian art: Everything about it is a "performance". The church has become a *theatrum sacrum*.

At the end of the Middle Ages, sculpture had interpreted the *tableaux vivants* of the mystery plays in quite a different spirit. Episodes of sacred history were inserted into the course of everyday life. It was a holiday, a lavish and popular "display", including naïve devices that were the delight of simple people. Mary Magdalene was shown as a Flemish courtesan, King Herod as a German baron, our Lady as a young lady or duenna, St Michael as a knight, St Jerome as a cardinal and God the Father as the pope. But in the new era of the Counter-Reformation, the function of art is no longer to make heaven come down to earth, but rather to lift up man's soul—or imagination—to the empyrean heaven.

To lift up man's soul. This explains the essentially *dynamic* character of such an art. The Byzantine mosaic or the tympanum of Moissac are, so to speak, final interpretations of the Beatific Vision. They force themselves on us with a kind of radiant, immobile indifference. They are what they are. Baroque staging is quite different: it *rises,* and the rays of divine glory are rungs on a Jacob's ladder, not rays of an eternal rainbow or of a fixed star. Everything contributes to this effect: the feeling of perspective in order to hollow out and breach the sky; the tricks of lighting which capture our eye; everything, in fact, makes an airy appeal. The favourite themes of this style are highly significant: ecstasies, assumptions, transfigurations.

The Middle Ages had interpreted the thrust towards God in a way that would henceforth be regarded as childish—through symbolic gestures, such as hands joined in prayer, the contortion of the apostles' or elders' necks before a divine manifestation, or the emergence from a dying person's mouth of a small doll representing the soul. Now *everything* must be in flight, and space itself becomes a kind of vast wind-tunnel. Garments swirl in a divine wind or a flutter of angels' wings. Gestures become fuller as if in response to an appeal from on high. And if, by chance, a saint's arms are clasped together, they may be seeking to restrain within the bosom a heart bursting with an excess of love, or they may be engaged in modestly adjusting the folds of garments disarrayed by the force of a storm sweeping the figure up to heaven. It is as if a sovereign magnet or lover[5]—were drawing everything to Him. And the impression sought is one of contagion so that, as the spectator beholds the upward glance of Mary, St Teresa or St Francis, he himself is impelled to soar towards the divine heights.

An astonishing example of this style is furnished by an "Assumption of the Virgin" (1722) at Rohr in southern Germany. It is the work of Asam (1692–1750), an artist from Munich who was trained in Italy. On the same level as the floor of the church, an apostle is shown arriving too late for the miracle. With expansive gestures other apostles call to him from the three steps that form the pedestal of Mary's tomb, telling him what has happened. Still other apostles are grouped around the empty grave, and one of them holds, in an eloquent gesture of surprise, a rose he has discovered. All display impetuous emotion over Mary's flight. The Virgin herself soars upwards with outstretched arms, sustained by a host of angels in a tumult of wings and draperies. At the highest plane, the Trinity summons and awaits her among the clouds. Illumination is an integral element in the grandiose "finale" of this complex piece of operatic staging. The light falls from above and the rear of the composition, apparently emanating from beyond God or from some well-placed projector.

In other examples, a dramatic dynamism seems to be trying to eliminate any stationary means of support. The work of sculpture floats between heaven and earth, depicting —as in Bernini's "Ecstasy of St Teresa"—the encounter between an ecstatic saint and an angel from the sky.

Such sculptors are showmen, dominating the group of actors they have created. Should we conclude from this that they bear no witness at all of God? Certainly, they "orchestrate" their subjects. But did not the creators of the royal

[5] *Translator's note:* The word *aimant* means both lover and magnet.

portal do likewise? The music here is different and so, too, is the libretto. But after all, both of these different kinds of creators interpreted plastically the theological notions of their times. For the artists of the Counter-Reformation, such notions are the decrees of the Council of Trent as well as the testimonials of mystics and spiritual leaders approved by the Church. This is the light in which we should envisage the themes these artists treated. They limited themselves to a few noble subjects, carefully selected because of their dogmatic importance in defending against Protestant attacks the sacraments, Mary's spotless dignity, the intercession of the saints, the efficacy of good works and the papacy.

That art seems haughty—and so it is—because it assumed the task of praising God and His servants *in a triumphal way*. Everything is viewed in terms of conquest—the conquest of souls by all the powers of heaven, and the conquest of heaven by all souls. The result is a kind of universal imperialism in the manner of Corneille's dramas, full of outbursts of zeal and grace, and theatrical gestures.

What this art extolls is not at all the peace promised to men of good will, but the victory of men of heroic determination. And doubtless that is why we feel alienated from all those saintly figures, who seem perpetually challenging us to reach the lofty status they have attained, even though they have done so in all humility.

Let us consider, for example, a statue of St Francis in the plastic polyphony of a great Spanish altar-screen. The saint kneels, eyes closed in ecstasy and hands extended. A dazzling visitation of God overwhelms and at the same time sustains him. Francis is bathed and suffused in gold; his habit is braided and worked in gold filigree, and the cord about his waist is gilded. Where, then, is the saint who devised in love the crib of Greccio and curbed the wolf of Gubbio? [6] What

[6] The animals—those old, gentle and brotherly companions of the saints, even if some of the animals were monsters—no longer

has happened to the Poverello's gentle kindness, to his humorous simplicity, to his fantastic docility and child-like spirit? The bad aspect of this kind of Christian sculpture—which explains why it makes Frenchmen feel particularly uneasy[7] —is not so much its solemnity and vast need for grandeur. Such art forgets that the kingdom of heaven is not only evoked in the brilliance of Mount Tabor but also in the parable of the woman who lost a drachma and found it again by sweeping her house. Such art does not allow holiness to keep two feet on the ground and radiate grace into everyday life.

We should not feel such art is insincere. Everything grandiloquent is not deceitful, and the Jews knew well that God's voice resounded in the thunder and lightning. But their religion forbade the making of images. The grandeur and also the danger of Baroque art lie in the desire to fix, *through images,* as if through a kind of exercise, the infinite splendour and power of God. The Jews accumulated riches for the Temple, but they left the Temple itself empty. Perhaps that was the only way to keep a profusion of treasures from striking a hollow note.

Let us start out with the concept that for God there can be no possibility of an *excess,* by definition, because whenever we speak of an excess we must speak of a limitation. Similarly, let us reflect that nothing can be too beautiful, too powerful or too rich for God. For we run the risk of forgetting that the fascinations and powers of art are always human— only too human—and that the only way our lowly earth's

---

had a place in the new iconography. Stories about them were regarded as suspect legends or examples of ridiculous familiarity. Such an attitude was due to the worst kind of humanism which no longer realized that all creatures are children of God and our brothers, and that this is not just their dignity but our own.

[7] See some admirably nuanced analyses of this point in *Baroque et classicisme* by V. L. Tapié.

speech can approach the fulness of God is not through a frenzied display of resources and energies, but through the achievement of a certain quality of silence and peace. That fact was known to the great artists of the twelfth and thirteenth centuries. And we may wonder which art work is after all more naïve and which tells us more about the supreme secret of eternal happiness—the little bas-relief of "The Ecstasy of Mary Magdalene" at Autun or "The Assumption of the Virgin" at Rohr. The latter only succeeds in leaving us gasping over its composition and dazzled by its details. Spiritual joy finds here neither its method of expression nor its summing-up.

*   *   *

All eyes were still—and continuously—turned towards Italy. That land went on exporting artists. Above all, no talented art beginner from all of Catholic Europe failed to go to Rome for training and for work, sometimes staying there for years. The young artist saw first of all the works of antiquity; he saw Michelangelo, and he saw Bernini.

Like the greatest of his predecessors, Gianlorenzo Bernini (1598–1680) was an architect as well as a sculptor. This could be felt only too clearly in his grandiose "indoor construction pieces", such as the pulpit and baldacchino of St Peter's in Rome or the tombs of the popes. Bernini's altars assume gigantic proportions.[8] The pulpits become frantic, and we may well ask what voice of thunder is needed for an orator to deserve those stormy compositions of clouds, rays, draperies, acorns, pompons, palms and garlands. A similar remark may be made about the organ-lofts. Everything is a pretext for sculpture to launch out in an assault on space, encumbering it in an ostentatious way. Bas-relief work was doubtless judged a bit paltry and thus less used. It is dis-

---

[8] For example, St Peter's in Rome; Val de Grâce in Paris; the altar of St Ignatius in the Gesù in Rome (1680) by Father Pozzo.

played, however, in tumbling groups of angels and the emblems of the cupola's pendentives, and it took on a surprising
vigour in stucco. At Santa Zita's in Palermo, for example,
Serpotta covered the entire inner surface of the walls with
it—a soft form of carving which makes possible at a lesser
cost the pride Bernini displayed when he boasted he had
"made marble as supple as wax".

The statues themselves[9] are only bravura pieces—but what
pieces after all! St Laurence undergoes martyrdom; David
clenches his lips and frowns as he balances a slingshot; St
Bibiana is in ecstasy; St Teresa is overwhelmed by a wound
of love; the Blessed Albertona expires in agony and ecstasy
—these are Bernini's subjects. The main figure feels a press-
ing need to attract attention to himself. "Longinus" in St
Peter's in Rome thrusts his lance and agitates his arms; even
his hair and beard are vehement. Mocchi's "Veronica"—
the statue next to the "Longinus"—is not more restrained.
Nothing is relatively calm except the allegorical figures fram-
ing the papal tombs; and the figure of Death on Urban VIII's
tomb, it must be admitted, is an eloquent and macabre display. It is worth noting that Bernini attempted a Madonna
and Child—that prime example of a peaceful subject—only
once, in Notre Dame of Paris.

It is easy to sum up quickly the results of this art-style.
Maderna, as a sculptor, used the light of his talent to restore
ancient works, but he is justly famous for his statue of the
dead St Cecelia (1600), which is so simple, chaste and
gracious in its flexibility. Alessandro Algardi (1602–1654)
seemed for a time even to rival Bernini in brilliance. But
Bernini outshone both artists by far. Some of Bernini's suc-
cessors, of course, sought to achieve effects through refine-

---

[9] The arrangement of the façades scarcely allowed for outdoor
sculptural decoration, apart from the colossal apostles which
A. Galilei placed atop St John Lateran in 1734. They are shown
in animated poses along with Christ.

ment rather than through power; one of these men—Valle
—was, next to Algardi, a virtuoso in bas-relief work. But in
any case, the spirit of virtuosity was in command. Marchiori's
"St Joseph", for example, does not lack nobility, but it is
mainly a study in the materials of drapery. Pierre Legros
(1656–1719) and Michel-Ange Slodtz (1705–1764)—the
first an Italianized Frenchman, the second an Italianized
Fleming; the Schiaffinos of Genoa; Spinazzi of Florence; and
Serpotta, Corradini and Sammartino of southern Italy: All
were rivals in ingenuity and emotionalism. As a result, we
have such subjects as "St Bruno" rejecting with an affected
pout the mitre and crosier offered to him by a cherub; the
agony of St Stanislas Kostka; and, in the church of the Gesù,
tableaux of "Faith Vanquishing Idolatry" and "Religion
Striking Heresy with a Lightning Bolt". Elsewhere are statues
of "Modesty" and "Faith" completely enveloped—heads as
well as bodies—in an allegorical veil that moulds their figures;
Christ is similarly portrayed in a winding sheet that reveals
his features. And finally, we have "Man Liberating Himself
from the Network of Error" with the help of a small, winged
genius and many symbolical accessories—a fantastic piece
by Queirolo in San Severo's in Naples. But what in thunder
is it doing in a church?

At the end of the century, Baroque art had run out of
breath—and God knows that it had had plenty! It could
charm the spectator when it was amusing and when it was
amusing itself. But all too often, its billowing monotony and
majestic and simpering manner condemned it beyond recall.
A reaction towards simplicity, based on a new return to the
art of antiquity, resulted in a vehement attack on the Baroque
style just prior to the French Revolution.

*   *   *

The Baroque style, indeed, had encountered opposition in
France as early as the seventeenth century. An indication

of this could be seen in Bernini's famous voyage to Paris, in 1665, which did not achieve the anticipated result of service for Louis XIV and Colbert.

Just as France had opposed the disheveled flamboyance which, in different ways, marked in Germany, England and Portugal the end of the Gothic style, she was hardly receptive to Bernini's excesses. France was not fond at all of agitated motion, and opposed it with the stability of the classical style and the stiffness of the academic tradition.

This does not mean that France had no acquaintance at all with the Baroque—for she knew about it quite early. In the time of Cardinal Mazarin, a fondness for the Italian style was in full swing and it inspired the pulpit in the church of St Étienne du Mont in Paris (1651), which was designed by Laurent de la Hire and carved in wood by Claude Lestocart. The central element of the pulpit is supported by a statue of Samson; panels of the stairway and balustrade show scenes from St Stephen's life, the Evangelists, Doctors of the Church and figures of Virtues. Angels swing from the canopy, and at the very top an angel in glory sounds the trumpet of Fame and of the Resurrection. Pierre Puget (1620–1694), who worked a great deal in Italy, carved in Genoa a "St Sebastian" and two versions of the "Immaculate Conception" worthy of Bernini. Later, Jean-Baptiste Lemoyne and Michel-Ange Slodtz (who has been mentioned previously) used polychrome marbles in compositions of a theatrical nature. Slodtz, his followers and the Adams brothers—Lambert-Sigisbert and Nicolas—were organisers of funeral ceremonies and also sculptors. In fact, the tombs of that period [10] resembled mountains because of their pyramids, columns, torsos, trophies, escutcheons, urns, braziers and declamatory figures. Yet, despite such displays of pomp, we can feel the discipline imposed by "good taste", as formulated and im-

[10] The masterpiece of this style was the tomb of Maurice of Saxony in the Protestant church of St Thomas in Strasbourg.

posed in the academic lectures of Charles le Brun, the painter. And it was according to le Brun's designs that François Girardon, André Coysevox and Jean-Baptiste Tuby carved figures on Cardinal Richelieu's tomb in the Sorbonne, Colbert's in the church of St Eustache and le Brun's mother's in the church of St Nicolas du Chardonnet. When Coysevox and Nicolas and Guillaume Coustou did over, in 1699, the choir of Notre Dame in Paris, they preserved a majestic serenity as they erected noble works in the Christian, monarchical tradition. All the sculptors of the Versailles school had an obvious concern for decorum if not for artistic restraint.[11] But in their relative sobriety, all the feminine figures of allegories adorning the altars, stair-ways and corridors of the palace and the walks of its park[12]—Virtues and Seasons as well as statues of Fame and Victory—become confused in the spectator's mind.

More interesting perhaps are examples of two frankly divergent trends. On one hand, we have the colossal "Assumption of the Virgin" by Bridan at Chartres (1773) as well as the pulpits and high altars piled up by the tumultuous zeal of Slodtz and his helpers; and on the other hand we find the gracious, if slightly soft and mannered "Madonna" of Chastel in the Madeleine of Aix and especially the "St Bruno" of Jean-Antoine Houdon in Santa Maria degli Angeli in Rome (1766). Houdon's work was perhaps the classical period's loveliest religious statue; in the midst of so many displays of ecstasy, excess, and posed elegance, "St Bruno" stands alone, motionless, upright, clothed in thick wool. The saint's eyes are closed—not so that he may die or swoon, but to enable him to meditate on God. This is something which is of no concern to other sculptured figures

---

[11] Let us not forget the influence exercised directly or indirectly by Jansenism in favor of austerity.

[12] Guillaume Coustou sculptured Marie Leczinska as both "Charity" and "June".

of the period, through some excess or default. It is the only statue of the time which has an inner life.

*   *   *

In Flanders, by way of contrast, we should mention such artists as François Duquesnoy, who later settled in Rome; the Verbruggens; Lucas Faidherbe, a pupil of Rubens; and Jean Delcour. They contributed huge, so-called confessional high altars which evoke anything other than the mood for examining one's conscience, confessing one's sins and contrition; they also offered elaborate thunderous pulpits, like the one in St Gudule's in Brussels. The full-blown decorative tradition of the Antwerpian reredos was torrentially engulfed in the new channel opened up by the development of the new style.

In Central Europe, the Germanic and Czech forms of the Baroque are particularly remarkable.[13] Just as elsewhere in Europe, the new style triumphed on altars and pulpits (for example, the pulpit at Krems in Austria); elaborate reredos (such as the one at Leoben in Austria); and imperial or princely tombs. In these lands where Catholicism was served in a propagandistic spirit, as a part of the reconquest of the area from Protestantism, all the fascination and intimidation the Baroque style can exercise are exploited to the full. Prelates, religious orders and rulers wished to place everywhere the mark of a triumphant Catholicism—not only in sanctuaries but also in secular places. In Bohemia and Austria, outdoor monumental sculpture flourished on castle terraces, bridge parapets and public squares. We find fountains and votive columns, like Linz' Column of the Trinity

[13] We should also include works erected in the Catholic cantons of Switzerland. In addition to the usual allegories, the most interesting pieces are monumental fountains; in the German tradition, they contain religious figures such as Moses striking the side of the cliff in search of water.

surmounted by a monstrance (1723); St Anne's Column in Innsbrück; or the Column of the Virgin in Graz.

In the Czech area, there are countless images of SS Wencelas, John Nepomucene and Florian. Everywhere the influence of Italian art was dazzling, particularly at Prague in the work of Ferdinand and Johann Brokoff and Mathias Braun (1684–1738).

Braun's best-known work is the St Luitgard group: The nude Christ wears a crown of thorns; His right hand is still nailed to the cross, while His left hand has been detached and tenderly touches Luitgard's shoulder; the saint herself embraces Christ's knees. Everything here is worthy of Bernini: the cascade of cherubs down the upright of the cross; the contrasting motions of Christ's inclined torso, the draperies, and the soaring windswept banner at the top of the cross with the inscription INRI. Among the Germans we should also mention Joseph Goetsch, J. A. Feuchtmayr (1696–1775) and Ignaz Günther, the last great rococo sculptor, whose "Pietà" of painted wood at Nenningen (1774) combines theatricality and elegance.

There remains only Spain, which during the seventeenth and eighteenth centuries was surely the domain of Christian sculpture's most dazzling flowering; and through Spain's empire this art had a world-wide extension. The influence of Italian art became noticeable in Spain during the last third of the sixteenth century. The Counter-Reformation here assumed no aspect of constraint, for it was at home in Spain, where the paganising Renaissance had never really taken root. There was no sharp break and no reaction between the "Baroque" tendencies of the late Middle Ages and the Baroque style that followed a Reformation which Spain had never known and a Michelangelo who had never been victorious here.

Until the end of the Baroque period, the Spaniards continued to carve statues of the "Virgin of Mercy", the "Virgin of Sorrow" and the "Dead Christ"—works which are much more closely connected to the tragic mediaeval tradition than the few macabre aspects of Bernini's style. All Spanish sculpture was directly religious; no concession was made to the hybrid genre of allegorical figures. Of course, such art was theatrical, but it served the theatre of the so-called liturgies of Holy Week when statues and groups of figures known as *pasos* were carried in procession through the streets.

The artist Juan Martínez Montañés, it is said, used to run from one crossroad of Seville to another to watch his statue of Christ carrying the Cross as it passed and repassed. Montañés had a boundless affection for this work, and God alone would have to discern how much human pride and how much humility was in the artist's soul. A fervent Christian, he took Communion each day before beginning to work. Another artist, Pedro de Mena, saw one of his sons become a Jesuit, another a diocesan priest, and three of his daughters nuns. The artist Salzillo was a Dominican, who was forced against his own inclination to resume the lay-state in order to provide for his widowed mother.

The subjects of Gregorio Hernandez (1566–1636) and Montañés (1568–1649) were closely related to the general condition of Spanish piety. They were themes of emotional devotion, such as the "Virgin of the Seven Swords"; the "Way of the Cross"; the head of John the Baptist; St Jerome as an old man engaged in acts of mortification; and St Dominic flagellating himself. They also depicted saints associated with the spread of great religious orders, such as Ignatius of Loyola, Francis Xavier, Francis Borgia, Francis of Assisi, Antony of Padua, Vincent Ferrer, Pedro de Alcántara, Teresa of Ávila, John of the Cross, John of God and Bruno.

The general trend was towards a violent expressionism that cultivated all means of capturing popular emotions;[14] and, in

[14] The souls of mystics were nourished on the same sources. It is

fact, such sculpture was the object of immense fervour. Under the direction of the great sculptors, art studios made countless copies of the most admired works.

Even in the middle of the eighteenth century, the people of Murcia believed that a supernatural hand had intervened in Salzillo's "Agony of Christ". For such a splendid creation seemed beyond merely human power. A convulsive, barbaric realism was developed. Statues with eyes of coloured glass wept crystal tears and were provided with real finger-nails, eyebrows and hair. In Burgos, a statue of Christ was fitted with human skin. Fleshy parts were painted in natural skin-tones with bluish or reddish wounds. And to convey a greater feeling of majesty and life-likeness, frequent use was made of statues described as *de vestir* (that is, designed to wear clothing),[15] which were covered with brocades, crowns and jewels. The penitent Magdalene was enveloped in a tunic of real reeds. In extreme cases, the sculpture was buried under fripperies of an ostentatious, yet popular, piety.

We are reminded of the ironic remarks made long ago by the theologian of Chartres concerning St Foy's image at Conques. But Spanish theologians apparently were concerned about the danger of "idolatry" only with respect to their flocks in America. The Third Council of the Church in Mexico decreed that images "should be paintings insofar as possible, or if they are carved images, let them be done in such a way that they do not have to be adorned with clothing".

All that sculpture was in polychrome wood.[16] The sculptor cut *en blanco,* which means that he left the wood bare. After him came the *incarnador,* then the *estofador,* who

---

known that St Teresa was influenced, in the sixteenth century, by a statue of the bleeding Christ before which she used to pray.

[15] For this purpose, statues were articulated, such as Juan de Mesa's "Christ of Great Power" at Seville. Often the sculptor handled only the unclothed parts of the body, *i.e.,* the hands and face.

[16] Only Alonso Cano of Grenada (1601–1667) worked in stone.

finished the work. Painters like Francisco Pacheco or Valdés Leal assumed this task, which was not regarded as inferior. As a rule, however, the different stages were handled within the same studio, which often was a family affair. In the sixteenth century, the veneering was brilliant and resembled enamelling. In works prepared in the Americas, this type of finish was in general retained. But Pacheco established the superiority of a dull shade of painting for the fleshy parts, because it was more realistic. Surfaces depicting fabrics were gilded and then overpainted; a punching process brought the gold to light again in order to imitate laminated or figured textures.

In addition to the statues, we should mention the reredos —vast compositions which, in the eighteenth century, sought to achieve a synthesis of architecture, sculpture and painting. The finest example of that art was the reredo (now destroyed) which the Tomes erected in León Cathedral. Christ was seated under a portico at the banquet table of the Last Supper, with two of his apostles; the other apostles were shown hurrying through real columns to take their places at His side.

We shall not go into more details concerning the huge output of statuary by such artists as Pedro de Mena (who died in 1693); Juan de Mora (whose life extended from 1642 to 1724 and was as tumultuous as his works); and Luís Roldan. If we examine the development of their art up to the early nineteenth century, we become convinced that this essentially was the origin of the dreadful, tasteless sculpture of modern times. After 1750, that taste in art was attacked by the academic tradition, which sought to achieve a greater austerity and generally abandoned religious sculpture. But labels are of little value in such matter: Whether we are concerned with Salzillo (1707–1783), Luís Carmona (1709–1766), or Lujan (1756–1815), who was active in the Canary Islands, we should realise that all three artists led directly to the worst kind of art. We may imagine that, if the taste of aesthetes should rehabilitate the work of these sculptors—as will happen inevitably some day—this will come about through the subterfuge of honouring them as sculptors. All we shall have to do is to leap over the barrier—a serious one, if the truth be told—of the abandonment by nineteenth-century art of every vestige of its lofty traditions, and the substitution of a vile, weak material—plaster—for the noble wood.

* * *

In all the territories ruled by Spain—from the Canary Islands to Cuba and the Philippines, including the Americas—sculpture flourished and bore fruit.[17] A decree of 1589 authorized natives of the Americas to collaborate with artists but only for decorative works, not for statues of saints. There were, however, several Indian sculptors: the Peruvians Yupanqui (whose "Virgin of Copacabana" dates from 1583); Tayro-Topa, who worked at Cuzco in the seventeenth century; and Gaspar Zangurrima, who worked at Quito around the end of the eighteenth century. Their works did not differ from those of Spanish artists, who were often members of religious orders, such as Father Carlos or the Carmelites of Quito. The art center at Quito exported its products all over Latin America, to the Canary Islands, and even to Spain itself.

The originality of Spanish colonial art[18] was in the façades, which were often thought of as large reredos in stone, decorated with colonnades and statues. Examples in Mexico are at Taxco, Zacatecas, Tepozotlan as well as the *Sacrario* of Mexico City. Inside decorations were even wilder than

[17] Portuguese art, in Brazil (Ouro Preto) and Goa, scarcely differed from the art of the Spanish territories.

[18] Cf. V. L. Tapie, *op. cit.,* pp. 300–323; Geo-Charles, *Art Baroque en Amerique Latine,* Plon, 1954.

those in the Iberian Peninsula, if we can imagine such a possibility. Examples are at Tanantzintla in Mexico and the Church of the Immaculate Conception at Recife in Brazil. Among devotional statues, we should mention the ones in Rio de Janeiro by "Master Valentine"—Valentine de Fonseca Silva. And we may leave the Baroque art of Latin America with the extraordinary achievement of a Brazilian mulatto, Alijadinho (1738–1814), the bastard son of a Portuguese artist. His twelve great statues of prophets stand in front of the Church of the Bom Jésu at Congonhas de Campo. The agitated figures are firmly carved in stone and reveal an eloquent and monumental power.

*　　*　　*

As we have just related, Iberian religious sculpture was a popular art. The greatest sculptors clung to the honour of making *pasos* for street processions. And they did not disdain to make crèches, such as the one by Salzillo (now in the museum of Murcia) containing no less than 556 human figurines and 373 animal forms, all in clay except for the wooden figure of the Baby Jesus. This work dates from 1780. We might also mention the Portuguese crèches of Mahado de Castro (1766), Joaquin de Barros and Antonio Ferreira. A fondness for such works originated in Italy, especially Naples, in connection with *tableaux vivants* set up inside chapels in such places as Varello, Orta, Varese and Oropa.[19] These compositions swarming with statuettes represent, against a background of painted decorations, the mysteries of the Rosary or scenes of the Passion; they were prepared throughout the sixteenth, seventeenth and eighteenth centuries. Such constructions can be directly traced back to the mystery plays of the Middle Ages, and the holy scenes offered a pretext for an outpouring of popular spirits—

[19] Cf. *L'Oeil*, November 1959.

bambochadas, as they are called in Spain. This same tradition is continued in our own day by the crèches of Provence.

Thus our attention is drawn to a most remarkable and continuous development—popular religious sculpture, which has not received sufficient investigation. It existed everywhere. Almost always anonymous, it was the work of local artisans, who were masons and carpenters as well as sculptors. They were people of slight inventive power who gave a hearty welcome to models reaching them from on high which they copied with different degrees of awkwardness. (Thus, in Brittany,[20] they were inspired by Flemish, Italian, Rhenish and Spanish art forms known to them, among other channels, through prints carried about by pedlars.) And there was a popular late Gothic style, extending from Hungary[21] to Portugal and from Ireland to Poland.

There was even a popular Baroque style throughout the Catholic world. The visitor who discovers so much "local colour" in the saints and reredos of crudely daubed wood in the Finistère region should realize that these works have close cousins in Auvergne, the valleys of the Alps and Pyrenees,[22] Italy, Spain, and as far away as Transylvania, Lithuania and Brazil.

That art is, however, astonishingly conservative, which accounts for its piquant "originality". In the mid-seventeenth century, the calvaries of Brittany displayed, in granite, scenes of the Passion in which the costumes worn are those of the mystery plays of Francis I's time. And nothing is more amusing about the reredos than the mixture of mediaeval candour and Baroque daintiness. With their fancy gilding

[20] Cf. Victor-Henry Debidour, *La Sculpture bretonne, étude d'iconographie religieuse populaire,* Rennes, 1953.

[21] Cf. A. Kampis, *Sculpture sur bois mediévale en Hongrie,* Budapest, 1940.

[22] Such popular works have suffered less destruction in remote regions as the result of the spread of the enlightenment and "good taste".

and colouring, such works spring directly out of a Christian community of peasants which is sly and rustic, frank and lusty, uniting as well as it can the awkwardness it preserves, the wealth it seeks and the simplicity it cherishes.

Here we ought to mention pell-mell—chronology is of slight importance in such art—the processional statues of southern Corsica;[23] wooden crucifixes erected along the highways of Austria and Rumania; "oratories" of Provence (all of which have lost their original statuettes); ceremonial staffs of brotherhoods, or religious societies, which are often adorned with religious insignia; and even pieces of furniture on which cabinet-makers would often carve Christian symbols.

Such minor works, although once numerous, have been decimated by many kinds of vandalism. But the tradition that spread them, especially between the sixteenth and eighteenth centuries, died out only in the nineteenth century. In France, it even managed to survive the Revolution, but it had received its death wound. Between 1825 and 1860, the expansion of communications and culture (or of what then claimed to be culture) made people in the parishes—for example, in Brittany—feel ashamed of the so-called ugly, naïve images inherited from their ancestors. The lapse of half a century—more or less—between the drying up of such popular art and the first, effective attempts to preserve the treasures of folklore was disastrous. That period of time was enough to empty churches, cemeteries and crossroads of fine religious decorations and replace them with a hideous, cumbersome hodge-podge, except for a few lucky spots which, however, were threatened by sectarianism, "modernization" and inertia. Once the thread was broken, it could not be mended again.

[23] Cf. G. Moraacchini, *Trésors oubliés des églises de Corse*, Hachette, 1959.

But a history of Christian sculpture has to make room for such "secondary" pieces, which are truly works of a Christian community. The calvaries of Brittany, the crosses with their carved figures, the Virgins of Mercy from the Finistère region; the granite carvings eaten away by lichens and time for the past two to four hundred years (it is sometimes difficult to estimate their age exactly)—all those monuments prove to anyone who has seen them that a peasant art can also create thrilling compositions strongly rooted in a feeling for beauty. Raised up above man's earth and beneath God's sky, they stand for Christmas, Good Friday and Easter; they stand for the whole cycle of the seasons and the cycle of the saints.

*   *   *

We shall choose a closing statement from an Italian crucifix of painted wood, one mentioned by the art critic Enzo Carli. It was discovered among the ruins of the basilica of San Bernadino after its destruction by bombs in 1944. Christ's sweet, sad face had burst open, but a piece of parchment was found inside containing a message from the sculptor, Lando de Pietro. He requested the Virgin Mary, St John the Baptist, St John the Evangelist and St Mary Magdalene (the last-named saint was described as *"amatrice di Jesù Cristo figliuolo di Dio"*) to lead him to God. All the saints were asked to protect the artist and his family "against the hand of the enemy of God". And he added: "Jesus, Jesus Christ, Son of the living God, have mercy on the whole human race!"

Here are the last words of Lando de Pietro's message: "In the year of Our Lord 1337, in January, this figure of the likeness of Jesus Christ, Son of the living and true God, was completed. It is He whom we adore—not this piece of wood."

Everything Christian sculpture has to say, everything it has been able to say as well as everything it has failed to say, is in this prayer and message that were hidden with God for six hundred years inside a master-work whose carver's name was formerly not even known.

CHAPTER VIII

THE NINETEENTH AND TWENTIETH CENTURIES

ELEANOR ANN COLLINS ANDERSEN

Christian sculpture since the end of the eighteenth century has seen the nineteenth century with virtually no religious sculpture at all, and the present twentieth century alive with new drive and vigour for Christian representation.

The nineteenth century was a period of Romanticism—a time when man looked only to the past for his inspiration. This lack of forward view is disturbing to us today, but to the man of the nineteenth century it was a means of escape. The past held the glories of Greece and Rome while his present only held the soot and grime of long hours in a factory or the upheaval of revolution.

The nineteenth century was a time of revolt—political as well as religious. The beginning of the century witnessed social groups within nations revolting against taxation and loss of civil rights.

America, with its independence gained during the latter part of the eighteenth century, was the inspiration for many European nations. France followed in America's foot-steps with its own fight against the aristocracy—the French Revolution. Russia freed her serfs. Germany won her freedom from Austria and the German people struggled to develop their own republic.

While all of Europe was involved in battling the imperialistic tyrant Napoleon, the United States was faced with the growing problems of the free and slave states which finally culminated in a bloody Civil War.

The entire Western world was deeply enmeshed in the Industrial Revolution, which was brought about by the development of scientifically conceived machines intent on increasing economic production and man's material wealth.

The Catholic Church of the nineteenth century was far from powerful. The Church was an authority, and the primary goal of the nineteenth century's Romantic creed was to revolt against authority.

The nineteenth-century period is the least inspiring in the history of religious art because the Industrial Revolution had created a new aristocracy based upon the emergence of the entrepreneurial class. This bourgeois or middle class had new wealth which, when added to their desire to appear cultured, was centered on the production of inferior classical sculpture. It was this middle class, not the Church, which now commissioned renowned artists of the period to design elaborate tombs, public statues and portrait busts.

The stress in the nineteenth century was on secular art but there existed in the mid-century a form of "sugary", sympathetic religious art manufactured in factories. This mass-produced form consisted of plaster toy-like statues and color lithographs depicting little-known events in the life of Christ. These religious articles were sponsored by many of the clergy and held close by the average church-goer even into the twentieth century. These articles were excellent teaching aids, for they told the Bible stories and the early life of Christ and the saints, but they gave the public a distorted picture of the glory and power of Christ. They made him appear weak— almost as if they were putting a weak Christ at the head of a weak Church.

The Church no longer needed to educate the rapidly growing literate masses through the pictorial use of stained glass, or stone tympanum or painted image. The church was now face to face with the newly educated middle class, which held the majority of the wealth.

The nineteenth-century Church refused much of the art of the past, and it failed to provide a new art to meet the present. The Church approved of the plaster saints perhaps because it could dictate to a manufacturer who was in business more easily than it could deal with the nineteenth-century artist who was working to express himself, not the orders of the Church. The artist turned his back on the doctrines and chose human relationship to express his religious feelings.

As industrial production increased, more stress was put on the measuring of success in terms of money. Romanticism protested against the materialism of the Industrial Revolution. In early centuries the Church or aristocracy cultivated the arts, and they were passed on as a tradition. The sculptor could express these traditions and be accepted.

The French Revolution and the Industrial Revolution led Christian art off on a road which had little or no contact with religion. In the nineteenth century the sculptor discovered markets more lucrative than the Church. These sculptors were more devoted to resurrecting styles from the past than to developing new forms of their own.

In the early nineteenth century Antonio Canova (1757–1822) decorated tombs and monuments with classical figures and angels. His works were done more in a decorative vein than centred on conveying any religious sentiment. Actually Canova's influence on younger artists was more outstanding than his religious sculpture. He was always willing to aid young artists either financially or in securing commissions for them. Canova was an excellent example of the early-nineteenth-century sculptor, an artist with great technical skill, working in the Romantic tradition, expressing himself through the past. Among his works are the monuments to Pope Clement XIV and Clement XIII.

Bertel Thorwaldsen (1768–1844) was one of the young artists whom Canova aided. His work can best be described as cold in its interpretation. Much of his work was executed by his students working from his models and plans. His tomb for Pius XII consisted of a colossal grouping of Christ and the Apostles for a church in Copenhagen. This work contained skill, but lacked true inspirational religious expression.

One nineteenth-century sculptor whose work showed true Christian feeling was the Englishman John Flaxman (1755–1826). Flaxman was basically a book illustrator, and, because of his interest in the linear, he was more concerned with relief sculpture. Flaxman held art to have an extremely high moral value. Due to his interest in the Italian works of the seventeenth century, he felt that his work, like the work of these earlier artists, should be directed towards the Church.

He decided to serve the Protestant Church as the Italians had served the Catholic Church. These Italian influences can be seen in his monuments. He would often include passages from the Bible on his monuments. These, along with ideals implicit in his work, gave a Christian touch to his monuments. But they still lacked the drive of religious fervour, for they were still representative of the skilful Romantic classical movement.

One sculptor who was capable of combining the classic with the dramatic-emotional feeling was François Rude (1784–1855). Rude's "Christ Crowned with Thorns" is a bust of Christ, utilizing the elements of the skilful craftsman. This is truly a religious subject, but the piece itself falls short on conveying the message of the crucifixion. The hair and beard are carefully executed, the thorns are extremely naturalistic but Christ seems almost serene, as if at rest.

There is nothing in the face of Christ that makes the viewer fully aware of the torture and suffering of Christ on the Cross. The spark of truth was growing but had not reached its culmination.

Augustus Saint-Gaudens (1848–1907), an American, was known for his large public monuments, symbolic figures and portraits. He designed some sculpture for churches, but his most outstanding work was the mourning figure designed for the Henry Adams tomb in Rock Creek Cemetery, Washington, D.C. The monument is austere in its simplicity. It consists of a lone, heavily draped bronze figure seated against a large block of granite. The drapery flows creating broad forms (not minute details). The head is covered with a cloth, and the quiet contemplative face peers from a pointed arch of material.

Saint-Gaudens' genius for the manipulation of light and shadow compels the viewer to keep looking at the figure and taking in the force of its mood of inner quiet. The figure has often been thought to be that of death, grief or divine peace, and although the true meaning of the figure is not known, one is immediately aware of the spiritually intense feeling this figure conveys. This work was a move towards a new representation: a representation of the times not of the elaborate classical past.

The skilful, realistic, classical representation became the ideal of nineteenth-century sculpture. But later in the century, the realistic was not suitable for some sculptors, who felt it was more important to convey the religious idea or content than the physical appearance. To these new sculptors it distracted from the beauty of the religious idea to have a too carefully conceived or "sugary" realistic representation.

At this point Auguste Rodin (1840–1917) appeared. He refused to work in the now over-used realism, and his knowledge of anatomy was masterful. He ignored the character of his materials; he manipulated bronze and stone so that it gave off a life and newness that religious sculpture had lacked for centuries.

He brought back feeling to sculpture rather than use it as just an illustrative element. Rodin sought new surfaces, new shapes, and new light effects. His influence was carried on by Bourdelle, Maillol, Matisse, and Modigliani—examples of only a few.

Rodin was opposed to classicism in sculpture because he was more interested in the representation of human emotions. One of his greatest pieces was "The Gate of Hell", which was commissioned in 1880 for the planned Musée des Arts Decoratifs. This large undertaking included a number of his well-known figures, among them "The Thinker".

Two sculptures which show that Rodin had the qualities of close observation and expressive symbolism are his "John the Baptist", powerful both in size and representation, and the symbolic hands, which he titled "The Cathedral". This piece is extremely expressive and symbolic. Rodin uses elongated hands, clasped and raised in prayer, emerging from the base of roughened stone as representing the cathedral. The elongation of the graceful hands gives one the feeling of the height and majesty of a Gothic cathedral reaching up from the earth with prayer to God.

At the height of Rodin's powers, and the beginning of the twentieth century, the Church was still no longer the chief patron of the arts, a position it had been losing since the Reformation and the French and Industrial Revolutions.

But in the twentieth century there appeared such a large number of artists, sculptors, painters and architects who have been working in a religious manner that it cannot be denied that a true Christian spirit is again growing in art.

This growing Christian artistic element has been aided by the work of Pope John XXIII and his successor Pope Paul VI. A basic change has been growing in the Church: a trend towards the complete participation of the people in the liturgy.

Art is not used in the liturgy of the Mass in the same manner as music is used; art plays no specific role. It is realized that the Church can exist without art, that man does not need it in order to save his soul. In the early days of the Church, works of art functioned as teachers of biblical stories, but now that the public has become more literate, this is no longer necessary. What then is the role of art in religion? How does the Christian artist play a part? The present-day artist works to express the meaning of the emotions which affect him as a human being in relation to his faith. He can work freely in a style of his own age without being confined by the styles of the past. Today, for the first time in years, the Church and the artist are moving with the modern age, not searching for something in the past. And they are both moving in the same direction—one which reflects the contemporaneity of the Church with art of a similarly modern conception.

At the conclusion of the second session of the Vatican Council, a Constitution of the Sacred Liturgy was published. Chapter Seven of this document is devoted specifically to the subject of art, and is entitled "Of Sacred Arts and Furnishings". The basic aim of the Vatican Council, stated in the Constitution's first chapter, was "to impart an ever-increasing vigour to the Christian life of the faithful". Therefore, Vatican II has kindled the flame that hopefully will grow into a raging fire—a fire that will breathe new life into Christian art.

Article 122 of the Constitution acknowledges that the Church is aware of her lost position as patron of the arts, and that she is now trying to return to that role. In Article 122 we read:

> Very rightly the fine arts are considered to rank among the noblest activities of man's genius, and this applies especially to religious art and to its highest achievement, which is sacred

art. These arts, by their very nature, are oriented towards the infinite beauty of God which they attempt in some way to portray by the work of human hands; they achieve their purpose of redounding to God's praise and glory in proportion as they are directed the more exclusively to the single aim of raising men's minds devoutly towards the Divine Majesty.

Holy Mother Church has always been the patron of the fine arts and has ever sought their valued help, with the special aim that all things set apart for use in divine worship should be truly worthy, becoming and beautiful, signs and symbols of the supernatural world. The Church has, indeed, trained artists and craftsmen to make such things. Moreover she has, with good reasons, reserved to herself the right to pass judgement upon the works of artists, deciding which of them are in accordance with faith, piety, and cherished traditional laws, and thereby fitted for sacred use.

The Church has been particularly careful to see that church furnishing should worthily and beautifully serve the dignity of workmanship, and has admitted changes in materials, style or ornamentation prompted by the progress of the technical arts with the passage of time.

Thus the Council makes it clear that the Church is very much interested in art and the work of today's artists. The artist of today might take objection to the Church's reservation of the right of judgement—and rightly so, if any priest or cleric who is not an informed art scholar simply declares the artist's work unfit. But in this statement the Council is speaking only of learned, informed appointees and groups who are striving for the very best work to be placed in the House of God, and who can best fight against the witless, sentimental plaster statues that have been filling the Church for more than one hundred years. These informed people are actually the true artist's most important ally, because they can protect the twentieth-century Church from returning to the past, as it did in the nineteenth century. This is further clarified in Article 122:

When passing judgement on works of art local ordinaries must listen to the opinions of the Diocesan Commission of

Sacred Art and—in those instances which call for it—also to those of others who are specially expert.

The last part of Article 122, which deals with Church acceptance of the new styles and materials, shows that she is aware of the new media which, through advances in science and technology, have become the tools of the artist. Such materials as plastic, synthetics, new metals and alloys are all accepted by the Church for use by today's sculptors.

In Article 123 we find the willingness of the Church to accept what is new:

> The Church has not adopted any particular style of art as her very own; she has admitted styles from every period according to the natural dispositions and circumstances of her peoples, and the needs of the various rites. Thus, in the course of the centuries, she has amassed a treasury of art which must be very carefully preserved. The art of our own days, coming from every race and region, is also to be given free scope provided that it adorns the sacred buildings and holy rites with due reverence and honour; thereby it is enabled to contribute its own voice to that wonderful chorus of praise in honor of the Catholic faith sung by great men in times gone by.

Here is the Church accepting and wanting today's art, not just Romanesque, Gothic and Renaissance. She also desires representation of the art of all the world's peoples and places.

One hopes that these precepts will encourage Christian missionaries to help develop and foster the art traditions of the people with whom they are working, and that they will stop imposing the sympathetic plaster statues and paintings of the nineteenth century on the peoples of Africa, China or India, for all these peoples have much artistic ability of their own with which to create a true Christian feeling in the styles of their own art.

In Article 124 we find more support for the artist—an implied reference to the positive quality of the use of simplicity.

Ordinaries, by the encouragement and favour they show to art which is truly sacred, should strive after noble beauty rather than sumptuous display. This principle is to apply also to sacred vestments and ornaments which ought not to be unduly expensive.

Bishops should carefully and insistently remove from churches and other holy places the works, produced by some artists, which do not accord with faith, morals and Christian piety, and which offend true religious sense either by depraved forms or by lack of artistic worth, mediocrity and pretense.

And when churches are to be built, ordinaries must see to it that the design of these churches is such as to facilitate the celebration of the liturgy and the active participation of the faithful.

In this article the artist is faced with some restrictions against unworthy art, but here again one feels that the Council is trying to protect the Church from the factory-produced statuary which is in the category of religious articles, not art.

In Article 124 the advice of the Diocesan Commission and experts is again implied. This wording is very loose; there are no real qualifications which could cage an artist or make him feel that the Church has placed too many obstacles in his way, restricting his ability to express his faith through his art.

François Rude's bust of "Christ Crowned with Thorns", mentioned earlier, is a representative piece of nineteenth-century classical Romantic sculpture. It exhibits all the realistic skill the artist possessed, but it did not bring to the viewer the harshness of the Cross. If we compare Rude's Crucifixion with the Crucifixion of the English contemporary sculptor Leslie Thornton, the viewer will see the marked differences between the realistic and the abstract version of the Cross. Through the use of welded bronze Thornton has created a framework of not one but many crosses. The figure of Christ emerges from the crossings of vertical and horizontal. The figure hangs, sagging from the weight of His body. Great thorns protrude from the head. This piece conveys the agony

of the Cross and all the sins of the world that put Him there.
This may be one reason for Thornton's use of many crosses
—a cross for each of man's sins.

One viewer might find Rude's Crucifixion pleasing and
Thornton's Crucifixion repellent to his faith and piety. But
does Thornton's repel his faith, or does it simply disturb him
because it strikes out at the truth that Christ suffered the
agony of an awful death on the Cross for our sins? It is
much more comfortable to gaze at the peaceful Christ in
polished marble or the pretty, painted plaster Christ than it
is to see suffering, which might make one think.

Article 125 of the Constitution reads:

> The practice of placing statues and pictures in churches so
> that they may be venerated by the faithful is to be main-
> tained; but their number should be moderate and their rela-
> tive positions should exemplify right order. For otherwise
> they might provoke astonishment among the people, and
> foster devotions of doubtful orthodoxy.

Here the Council stresses that people must be willing
to learn new ideas and concepts, to try to understand that
which is contemporary, and to learn what is art as opposed
to what is a dime-store religious article. The Church wants
the people to see values, to be able to see mediocrity, recognize it and keep it from·creeping into the Church. In Article
127 we read:

> Bishops should have a special concern for artists, so as to
> imbue them with the spirit of sacred art and of the sacred
> liturgy. This they may do in person, or through suitable
> priests who are gifted with a knowledge and love of art.
> It is also very desirable that schools or academies of sacred
> art should be founded in those parts of the world where they
> would be useful, so that artists and craftsmen may be trained.
> All artists who, prompted by their talents, desire to promote
> God's glory in the Church, should ever bear in mind that they
> are engaged in a kind of holy imitation of God the Creator,
> and are concerned with works destined to be used in Catholic

worship, to edify the faithful, and to foster their piety and their religious formation.

Both the foregoing and Article 129, which follows, are of particular importance both to the Church and to art.

During their philosophical and theological studies, clerics are to be taught about the history and development of sacred art, and about the basic principles governing the production of its works. In consequence they will be able to appreciate and preserve the Church's ancient monuments, and be in a position to aid, by good advice, artists who are engaged in producing works of art.

The education of the young and of future priests in art history and contemporary art is vital to the Church. With the huge growth taking place in parishes the world over and the call for new parishes, new schools and new churches, the priests need to have a knowledge concerning contemporary architecture, sculpture and painting. These priests will be directly involved as pastors and assistants in producing a Church of today that represents to the twentieth-century man the Glories of God and His Church.

The young seminarian who exclaims today that he has so much to study now, how can he fit in art? will be very glad that he did study art, for he will never be like the pastor who had a new and beautiful church and wanted to place a Gothic tapestry behind the simple, sharp-lined black and white altar! The seminarian should see the need for and value of this knowledge.

The Vatican Council II, with its far-reaching goals, may truly create once again a lasting relationship between the Church and art. With this discussion of Vatican Council II and with some idea of the sculpture of the nineteenth century as a reference guide, we can now approach the work of the twentieth-century sculptor.

As noted before, during the twentieth century a new drive for Christian representation had sprung forth. Modern sculptors have been able to look to the past in cases where the Church and its art were valid for inspiration, but they have been astute enough to see things for their true value. This allows the sculptor to choose from the past the Christian sculpture that is true and to disregard that which is false. During this century the sculptor has also become affected by a strong spiritual element which has driven him to create religious works without any visual influence other than his own drive of faith.

One of this century's sculptors who worked under Christian influence was Sir Jacob Epstein (1880–1959), an American by birth who lived the greater part of his life in England. Epstein's sculpture is usually of monumental size, and so is usually displayed in public places. Because his work is viewed by many, controversy has at times erupted over his unusual means of representation.

Take, for example, Epstein's "Adam". This large stone sculpture was a strange concept for the public of the late 1930's to comprehend because it was strange to see the world's first man depicted as anything but Anglo-Saxon. "Adam" is a strong, moving piece of sculpture, with an upturned face searching for light and truth. But Epstein's "Adam" bore the reflection of ancient Aztec or Inca sculpture.

This sort of innovation has been slowly moving into Christian concepts, and has even been recognized in Vatican Council II: Christ is not merely one type of man or of any particular race; He is, after all, a little of all men.

Epstein's "Madonna and Child" (1952) which was commissioned for the Convent of the Holy Child, London, illustrates the artist's powers of the use of scale and simplicity. This piece is of cast-lead and is simply fastened to the surface of the building, not resting on any base. The feet of both figures are pointed down, again illustrating Epstein's use of past influences: This time the Byzantine figures with downward-pointed feet come to mind. The Madonna and Child are covered with an almost skin-like material which binds and weighs them down. Yet the dynamic element is the manner in which the Child flings out his arms, expressing the vital thrust of Christ on the world. This same force and power is present in Epstein's other works including "Majestas", "The Visitation", with its extreme sensitivity, and his "Christ".

The work of Ernst Barlach (1870–1938) exhibits a stress on the simple, monumental sculptural form. Barlach was greatly influenced by German mediaeval wooden sculpture, and he often employed wood as a media. Even his bronzes with their flat simple plains seem to have a quality of carved wood. His bronze "Hovering Angel", a monumental eight-foot piece which is in the Church of Saint Antoine at Cologne, is suspended from the ceiling instead of being firmly anchored to the floor. Designed by Barlach in 1927 to be a war memorial, it now hovers over the graves of soldiers of two wars.

Barlach's "Flight into Egypt" and "Death" exhibit his interest in creating groups of figures united by one encompassing element. In his "Flight into Egypt", Saint Joseph's cape is used to create unity, for it is impossible to tell where the cape and Saint Joseph begin or end: They are one in their protection of the Blessed Mother and Child. This moving sculpture, showing Saint Joseph in his role of the protector, is only twelve inches high, yet it possesses force and strength similar to that of Barlach's eight-foot angel. Barlach's work further stresses the twentieth century's movement towards the truly expressive element of Christian faith.

The Englishman Henry Moore (1898–   ) has in his work represented the time-honoured theme of mother and child and the family. Moore's manipulation of the elements of form, mass, space and texture is always present in his work. His "Madonna and Child", for the Church of Saint Matthew at Northampton, England, shows a strength produced by its quality of roundness. The sculpture is of stone and like a good many of his works it is monumental in size. The recurring element of roundness in the piece is stressed in the shape of the heads of both mother and child, in the round shoulders and knees, and it unites the two figures, making them appear as one.

Moore's family groups seem to stem from the Christian theme of the Holy Family. In his family groups, whether stone or bronze, the same quality of unity can be seen. His family sculptures, with their graceful flowing lines leading from the man and wife to the child in the centre, seem to stress the importance of the family in today's culture as the center of Christian unity.

Another sculptor who portrays the family as well as executing outstanding religious portraits is the American William Zorach (1887–1967). Zorach's "The Family" is not as light and flowing as Moore's work, for Zorach represents his family almost as one. Its three members are gathered close together to give even greater feeling of unity. The "Head of Christ", "Moses" and "John the Baptist" clearly show Zorach's great strength and power in his representations. His style is simple and direct: He does not dwell on detail. He combines the textures of polished and roughened stone to create a strong quality, as seen, for example, in his "Head of Christ". This strengthening of Christ's image, a movement of the twentieth century, is part of a stirring to destroy the sentimental image created in the nineteenth century.

The twentieth century has also produced sculptors whose work is not basically of a religious nature, yet who have produced a number of sculptures that exhibit a particular religious element. One such artist is Jacques Lipchitz (1891–   ), who since 1940 has produced some pieces which have strong religious feeling. "Notre Dame de Liesse" (Our Lady of Joy), which was commissioned for the church at Assy, is one such example. This bronze sculpture has a very appealing serene and flowing quality about it. All its lines seem to flow from and around the Virgin Mother, emphasizing her unity with man.

Germaine Richier (1904–1959) was another artist whose greatest works were not in the realm of religious sculpture. There is a very different, grotesque quality about her work, and her subjects deal mostly with the nature of unappealing insects or animals like the spider and bat. Her work possesses the quality of unpleasantness: It has a feeling of decay about it. In her controversial sculpture "Christ", for the church at Assy, the viewer is faced with a representation which, because of its startling, mask-line qualities, is frightening and difficult to comprehend. Germaine Richier's means of depicting her "Christ" is not pretty and round, but hollow from His suffering.

The sculpture of the Englishwoman Barbara Hepworth (1903–   ) is of a geometric nature, centred upon the representation of the abstract and non-objective. Her six-foot-high sculpture "Cantate Domino" (Sing to the Lord), truly non-objective, has planes which rise from the base, moving in and up as one's song or prayer would rise up to God. This piece brings to mind Rodin's "Cathedral": In the place of the praying hands are the slender graceful planes rising up in the same manner towards God.

This brief history must yet deal with the development of Christian art among the missions. The most outstanding and challenging area is the fastest developing area of the world, Africa. In the past ten years new and independent nations have been emerging there, and so Africa is an excellent proving-ground for Vatican II's statement dealing with the acceptance of the art of different races and regions in Christian representation. It is exciting to think of the results that can occur if the Church and the artist start out with a clear understanding one for the other.

Such institutions as the School of Fine Arts of Makerere

College (Kampala Uganda), which is part of the University of East Africa, are secular bodies which in the past few years has been trying to bring the African art student to express himself through his own culture not through the culture of European man. This, of course, is all new and just in the beginning stages. The missionary must help rid the African Church of the sentimental religious ideas of the nineteenth-century European and replace them with a religious art which is representational of the African, and his culture. This will prove to be a great asset for the Church in Africa, for when the people see the Church and its teachings illustrated in terms they understand, they will be better able to adopt its teachings and truths. Christian art in the Africa of today could play as important a role in the teachings of the Church as it did in the Europe of the Middle Ages.

George Bandele is a twentieth-century African sculptor whose work illustrates the drive for Christian representation through a true African interpretation. Bandele has learned to express himself and his own religious feelings as an African.

One of his pieces most illustrative of this is his wood sculpture titled "A Magi". This piece is a very simple and direct statement of an old Christian theme rendered with much strength and expression. Bandele has given his Magi the stature of a great Benin king riding to pay honour to an even greater King, Christ.

The twentieth century has seen the new growth in Christian art. All artists, including sculptors, have learned to be honest and express their faith and themselves—not just the ideas of the past. Today's artist is a living artist—one who interprets his culture and faith for the glory and truth of a living God.

BIBLIOGRAPHY

BUCKLE, Richard. *Jacob Epstein, Sculptor.* Cleveland: World, 1963.

CRICHTON, J. D. *The Church's Worship: Considerations on the Liturgical Constitution of the Second Vatican Council.* New York: Sheed and Ward, 1964.

GETLEIN, Frank and Dorothy. *Christianity in Modern Art.* Milwaukee: Bruce, 1961.

LAUCK, Rev. Anthony. "What the Council Had to Say About Art", *Liturgical Arts,* Volume 32, No. 4, (August 1964), pp. 111–114.

Liturgical Arts, Volume 26, Nos. 3 and 4 (May 1958).

McCLINTON, Katharine Morrison. *Christian Church Art Through the Ages.* New York: Macmillan, 1962.

McCURDY, Charles (ed.). *Modern Art: A Pictorial Anthology.* New York: Macmillan, 1958.

MAILLARD, Robert. *Dictionary of Modern Sculpture.* New York: Tudor, 1960.

SCHAEFER-SIMMERN, Henry. *Sculpture in Europe Today.* Berkeley and Los Angeles: University of California Press, 1955.

SEUPHOR, Michel. *The Sculpture of This Century.* New York: George Braziller, 1961.

SWEENEY, James Johnson (ed.). *African Negro Art.* New York: The Museum of Modern Art, 1935.